Better Homes and Gardens®

so-easy
slow cooker

Meredith® Books
Des Moines, Iowa

Better Homes and Gardens® So-Easy Slow Cooker
Contributing Editor: Cathy Long
Contributing Designer: Angie Haupert Hoogensen
Copy Chief: Doug Kouma
Copy Editor: Kevin Cox
Editorial Assistant: Sheri Cord
Book Production Manager: Mark Weaver
Contributing Proofreaders: Terri Fredrickson,
    Abbie Hansen
Contributing Photographers: Marty Baldwin, Scott Little,
    Blaine Moats
Test Kitchen Director: Lynn Blanchard
Test Kitchen Product Supervisor: Jill Moberly
Test Kitchen Culinary Specialists: Marilyn Cornelius,
    Juliana Hale, Maryellyn Krantz, Colleen Weeden,
    Lori Wilson
Test Kitchen Nutrition Specialists: Elizabeth Burt, R.D., L.D.;
    Laura Marzen, R.D., L.D.

Meredith® Books
Editorial Director: John Riha
Deputy Editor: Jennifer Darling
Managing Editor: Kathleen Armentrout
Brand Manager: Janell Pittman
Group Editor: Jan Miller
Associate Design Director: Erin Burns
Director, Marketing and Publicity: Amy Nichols
Executive Director, Sales: Ken Zagor
Director, Operations: George A. Susral
Director, Production: Douglas M. Johnston
Business Director: Janice Croat

Vice President and General Manager, SIM: Jeff Myers

Better Homes and Gardens® Magazine
Editor in Chief: Gayle Goodson Butler
Deputy Editor, Food and Entertaining: Nancy Wall Hopkins

Meredith Publishing Group
President: Jack Griffin
President, Better Homes and Gardens: Andy Sareyan
Vice President, Corporate Sales: Michael Brownstein
Vice President, Manufacturing: Bruce Heston
Vice President, Consumer Marketing: David Ball
Director, Creative Services: Grover Kirkman
Consumer Product Marketing Director: Steve Swanson
Consumer Product Marketing Manager: Wendy Merical
Business Director: Jim Leonard

Meredith Corporation
Chairman of the Board: William T. Kerr
President and Chief Executive Officer: Stephen M. Lacy

In Memoriam: E.T. Meredith III (1933–2003)

All of us at Meredith® Books
are dedicated to providing
you with information and
ideas to enhance your home.
We welcome your comments
and suggestions. Write to us
at: Meredith Books Editorial
Department, 1716 Locust St.,
Des Moines, IA 50309-3023.

Cover Photography:
Front cover: Country Italian
Beef (page 9)
Photographer:
Kritsada Panichgul

Our seal assures you that every
recipe in *So-Easy Slow Cooker*
has been tested in the Better
Homes and Gardens® Test
Kitchen. This means that each
recipe is practical and reliable,
and meets our high standards of
taste appeal. We guarantee your
satisfaction with this book for
as long as you own it.

As calendars fill up, it gets harder and harder to find the time to enjoy family meals together. The recipes in *So-Easy Slow Cooker* can help you ease that dinnertime crunch. All it takes is a slow cooker and this versatile collection of recipes, and you're on the way to preparing delicious meals that simmer for hours and are ready to serve in minutes at the end of the day. Each one of the more than 200 exceptional recipes has been tested in the Better Homes and Gardens® Test Kitchen to guarantee that it works perfectly and is practical for today's families.

You'll find main dishes for every taste—from beef, pork, and lamb entrées to poultry, fish, and meatless recipes. Plus, slow-simmering side dishes and appetizers are ready to tote to potlucks or serve at parties. And to make meal planning easy, you can take advantage of the three bonus chapters that showcase quick salads, breads, and desserts to round out slow cooker meals. If you have questions about slow cooking, read pages 6 and 7 for helpful information.

With the creative ideas in *So-Easy Slow Cooker*, you'll always have the help and inspiration you need to fit satisfying home-cooked meals into your busy family's routine.

—*Lynn Blanchard*
Better Homes and Gardens®
Test Kitchen Director

contents
so-easy slow cooker

143

170

80

173

slow-cooker **basics**

With the help of a slow cooker, you can serve hearty, home-style meals whenever you like. Keep these practical pointers in mind to make the most of this versatile, timesaving appliance.

Types of Slow Cookers

When you shop for a slow cooker, you'll find two types—continuous and multipurpose. The recipes in this book were tested with a continuous slow cooker. It has heating coils that wrap around the sides of the unit (see photo, below) and remain on when the cooker is in operation. Usually there are two fixed heat settings—low (about 200°F) and high (about 300°F). Some models also have an automatic setting that shifts from high to low during use. Many models have removable liners.

Multipurpose slow cookers have heating elements located below the food containers and dials that indicate cooking temperatures. Because these units cycle on and off, the recipes in this book will not cook properly in these cookers.

What Size is Best?

The size of slow cooker you need depends on the number of people you plan to serve. That's why some cooks own several sizes. For one or two servings, the small 1½-quart size works best. It's also handy for keeping appetizers and dips warm at parties. The intermediate 3½- to 4½-quart cooker typically simmers enough to serve three or four. If you have a larger family of five to seven people or want to cook enough for two meals, look for a 4½- or 5-quart cooker. And if you frequently cook for eight or more, you may want to invest in a 6- to 8-quart model.

Avoid Switching Sizes

If you don't have the size of slow cooker called for in a recipe, it's important not to substitute a smaller or larger size. To work most efficiently, a slow cooker must be at least half but no more than two-thirds full. That's because the heat comes from the coils around the sides, not on the bottom. Most of the recipes in this book give a range of cooker sizes (such as 3½- or 4-quart). Be sure to use one that's within the range so the food cooks to the right doneness within the time listed.

Plan Ahead

Because you'll want to start many slow-cooker recipes early in the day, you can eliminate some breakfast-time hassles by preparing ingredients the night before. Here are a few dos and don'ts:

- Chop vegetables and refrigerate them in separate containers. (You can keep cut-up potatoes from turning brown by covering them with water.) Or if your cooker has a removable liner, place the vegetables in the liner, cover it, and keep it in the refrigerator until the next morning.

- Assemble, cover, and chill liquid ingredients or sauces separately from the solids.
- If you'd like to brown ground meat or poultry and bulk sausage the night before, be sure to cook it completely. Then store it tightly covered in the refrigerator. Don't brown roasts, cubed meat, or poultry pieces ahead because browning doesn't cook the meat or poultry completely through.

Adapting Family Recipes

If you'd like to convert a favorite recipe from conventional directions to a slow-cooking method, follow these guidelines:

- Select a recipe that uses a less-tender meat cut, such as pork shoulder or beef chuck, which usually requires long cooking. You'll need to experiment with recipes that use dairy products because they can break down during extended cooking. If you like, stir in cream, sour cream, or cheese just before serving.
- Then find a recipe in this book that's similar to your recipe to use as a sample. It will give you a feel for quantities and liquid amounts.
- Cut vegetables into pieces similar in size to those in the sample recipe; place them in the cooker.
- Trim fat from the meat and, if necessary, cut the meat to fit the cooker. Place it on top of the vegetables.
- Because liquids don't boil away as they do in conventional cooking, reduce the liquids in the original recipe by about half (except those dishes containing rice).
- Follow the heat settings and cooking times listed in the sample recipe.

Country Italian Beef

meaty
main dishes

When it comes to hearty, satisfying meals,

it's hard to beat these beef, pork, and lamb favorites. There's everything from Beef Goulash and Mexican-Stuffed Sweet Peppers to Tomato-Sauced Pork Chops and Moroccan Lamb to tempt you.

Country Italian Beef

Fennel and basil are an appealing change of pace in this bold-flavored beef stew.

Prep: 25 minutes **Cook:** 8 to 10 hours (low) or 4 to 5 hours (high)

Makes 6 to 8 servings

- 2 **pounds boneless beef chuck**
- 8 **ounces tiny new potatoes, halved or quartered**
- 2 **medium carrots or parsnips, peeled and cut into 1- to 2-inch pieces**
- 1 **cup chopped onion**
- 1 **medium fennel bulb, trimmed and cut into ½-inch-thick wedges**
- 1 **14-ounce can beef broth**
- 1 **cup dry red wine or beef broth**
- 1 **6-ounce can tomato paste**
- 2 **tablespoons quick-cooking tapioca**
- 1 **teaspoon dried rosemary, crushed**
- ½ **teaspoon ground black pepper**
- 4 **cloves garlic, minced**
- 1 **to 2 cups fresh basil leaves, fresh spinach leaves, or torn fresh escarole**

1. Trim fat from meat. Cut meat into 2-inch pieces. Set aside.

2. In a 4- to 5-quart slow cooker, combine potatoes, carrots, onion, and fennel. Add meat.

3. In a medium bowl, combine broth, wine, tomato paste, tapioca, rosemary, pepper, and garlic. Pour over mixture in cooker.

4. Cover and cook on low-heat setting for 8 to 10 hours or on high-heat setting for 4 to 5 hours. Just before serving, stir in basil.

Per serving: 319 cal., 6 g total fat (2 g sat. fat), 89 mg chol., 596 mg sodium, 23 g carb., 4 g fiber, 36 g pro.

Keep the Lid On

When something is cooking in a slow cooker, resist the temptation to lift the lid. The domed lid allows condensation to run down inside, forming a water seal that keeps in heat. Removing the lid allows the heat to escape and it takes the cooker a long time to build the heat back up. Slow-cooker recipes shouldn't need stirring, but if you need to add ingredients, replace the lid quickly. If you lift the lid without being instructed to do so, add about 30 minutes to the cooking time.

Southwest Steak and Potato Soup

Salsa is the key to the sensational flavors in this soup. Create your own "house" version by using your favorite kind.

Prep: 25 minutes
Cook: 8 to 10 hours (low) or 4 to 5 hours (high)
Makes 6 servings

1½	pounds boneless beef sirloin steak, cut 1 inch thick
2	medium potatoes, cut into 1-inch pieces
2	cups loose-pack frozen cut green beans
1	small onion, sliced and separated into rings
1	16-ounce jar thick and chunky salsa
1	14-ounce can beef broth
1	teaspoon dried basil, crushed
2	cloves garlic, minced
	Shredded Monterey Jack or Mexican blend cheese (optional)

1. Trim fat from meat. Cut meat into 1-inch pieces. Set aside.

2. In a 3½- or 4-quart slow cooker, combine potatoes, green beans, and onion. Add meat. In a medium bowl, stir together salsa, broth, basil, and garlic. Pour salsa mixture over meat and vegetable mixture in cooker.

3. Cover and cook on low-heat setting for 8 to 10 hours or on high-heat setting for 4 to 5 hours.

4. If desired, sprinkle individual servings with shredded cheese.

Per serving: 206 cal., 4 g total fat (1 g sat. fat), 68 mg chol., 624 mg sodium, 16 g carb., 3 g fiber, 27 g pro.

Beef Goulash

Depending on how much heat you like, choose sweet or hot Hungarian paprika to spice this goulash.

Prep: 25 minutes
Cook: 8 to 9 hours (low) or 3½ to 4½ hours (high), plus 30 minutes on high
Makes 6 servings

1½	pounds beef stew meat
2	medium carrots, bias-cut into ½-inch-thick slices
2	medium onions, thinly sliced
3	cloves garlic, minced
1¼	cups beef broth
1	6-ounce can tomato paste
1	tablespoon Hungarian paprika
1	teaspoon finely shredded lemon peel
½	teaspoon salt
½	teaspoon caraway seeds
¼	teaspoon ground black pepper
1	bay leaf
1	red or green sweet pepper, cut into bite-size strips
	Hot cooked noodles
	Dairy sour cream or yogurt
	Hungarian paprika (optional)

1. In a 3½- or 4-quart slow cooker, combine meat, carrots, onions, and garlic. In a small bowl, combine broth, tomato paste, the 1 tablespoon paprika, the lemon peel, salt, caraway seeds, black pepper, and bay leaf. Stir into vegetable and meat mixture in cooker.

2. Cover and cook on low-heat setting for 8 to 9 hours or on high-heat setting for 3½ to 4½ hours.

3. If using low-heat setting, turn to high-heat setting. Stir in sweet pepper. Cover and cook for 30 minutes more. Discard bay leaf. Serve with noodles. Top with sour cream. If desired, sprinkle with additional paprika.

Per serving: 356 cal., 11 g total fat (4 g sat. fat), 85 mg chol., 678 mg sodium, 33 g carb., 4 g fiber, 32 g pro.

Tender pieces of beef, carrot, onion, and sweet pepper simmer in a luscious **paprika- and caraway-accented** tomato sauce in this slow-cooker rendition of the old-world **classic.**

Beef Goulash

German-Style Beef Roast

Red wine, chopped dill pickles, and hearty mustard set this succulent beef pot roast apart from the rest.

Prep: 25 minutes
Cook: 8 to 10 hours (low) or 4 to 5 hours (high)
Makes 8 servings

- 1   2½- to 3-pound boneless beef chuck pot roast
- 1   tablespoon cooking oil
- 2   cups sliced carrot
- 2   cups chopped onion
- 1   cup sliced celery
- ¾   cup chopped kosher-style dill pickles
- ½   cup dry red wine or beef broth
- ⅓   cup German-style mustard
- ½   teaspoon coarsely ground black pepper
- ¼   teaspoon ground cloves
- 2   bay leaves
- 2   tablespoons all-purpose flour
- 2   tablespoons dry red wine or beef broth
     Hot cooked spaetzle or cooked noodles
     Snipped fresh parsley (optional)

1. Trim fat from meat. If necessary, cut meat to fit in a 3½- or 4-quart slow cooker. In a large skillet, brown the meat slowly on all sides in hot oil.

2. In the cooker, combine carrot, onion, celery, and pickles. Place the meat on top of the vegetables. In a small bowl, combine the ½ cup red wine, the mustard, pepper, cloves, and bay leaves. Pour over meat and vegetables in cooker.

3. Cover and cook on low-heat setting for 8 to 10 hours or on high-heat setting for 4 to 5 hours.

4. Transfer meat to serving platter; cover to keep warm. For gravy: Transfer vegetables and cooking liquid to a 2-quart saucepan. Skim off fat. Discard bay leaves. In a small bowl, stir together flour and the 2 tablespoons red wine. Stir into mixture in saucepan. Cook and stir over medium heat until thickened and bubbly. Cook and stir for 1 minute more. Slice meat. Serve with vegetables, gravy, and hot cooked spaetzle. If desired, sprinkle with parsley.

Per serving: 372 cal., 25 g total fat (9 g sat. fat), 82 mg chol., 414 mg sodium, 10 g carb., 2 g fiber, 24 g pro.

Hearty Beef Chili

Prep: 20 minutes
Cook: 9 to 10 hours (low) or 4½ to 5 hours (high)
Makes 8 to 10 servings

- 1½   pounds beef chuck pot roast, cut into 1-inch cubes
- 2   cups low-sodium vegetable juice or tomato juice
- 2   cups chopped onion
- 2   15- to 16-ounce cans black, red kidney, and/or garbanzo beans (chickpeas), rinsed and drained
- 1   14½-ounce can no-salt added diced tomatoes, undrained
- 1½   cups chopped green sweet pepper
- 1   10-ounce can diced tomatoes and green chile peppers, undrained
- 1   teaspoon ground chipotle chile pepper
- 1   teaspoon ground cumin
- 1   teaspoon dried oregano, crushed
- 3   cloves garlic, minced

1. In a 4½- to 6-quart slow cooker, combine meat, vegetable juice, onion, drained beans, undrained tomatoes, sweet pepper, undrained tomatoes and green chile peppers, ground chipotle chile pepper, cumin, oregano, and garlic.

2. Cover and cook on low-heat setting for 9 to 10 hours or on high-heat setting for 4½ to 5 hours.

Per serving: 226 cal., 4 g total fat (1 g sat. fat), 50 mg chol., 467 mg sodium, 27 g carb., 8 g fiber, 26 g pro.

German-Style Beef Roast

Mediterranean Pot Roast

Prep: 25 minutes
Cook: 10 to 11 hours (low) or 5 to 5½ hours (high)
Makes 8 servings

- 1 **3-pound fresh beef brisket**
- 3 **teaspoons dried Greek or Italian seasoning, crushed**
- 2 **medium fennel bulbs, trimmed, cored, and cut into thick wedges**
- 1 **14½-ounce can diced tomatoes with basil, garlic, and oregano, undrained**
- ½ **cup beef broth**
- ¼ **cup pitted green and/or ripe olives, drained**
- ¾ **teaspoon salt**
- ½ **teaspoon finely shredded lemon peel**
- ¼ **teaspoon ground black pepper**
- ¼ **cup cold water**
- 2 **tablespoons all-purpose flour**
  Hot cooked pasta or rice (optional)

1. Trim fat from meat. If necessary, cut meat to fit into a 5- to 6-quart slow cooker. Sprinkle meat with 1 teaspoon of the Greek or Italian seasoning. Place meat in the cooker. Top with fennel wedges.

2. In a medium bowl, combine undrained tomatoes, broth, olives, salt, lemon peel, pepper, and the remaining 2 teaspoons Greek seasoning. Pour over meat and vegetables in cooker.

3. Cover and cook on low-heat setting for 10 to 11 hours or on high-heat setting for 5 to 5½ hours.

4. Remove meat from cooker, reserving cooking liquid. Thinly slice meat. Arrange meat and vegetables on a serving platter. Cover meat and vegetables; keep warm. Pour cooking liquid into a glass measuring cup; skim off fat.

5. For sauce: Measure cooking liquid; add water if necessary to make 2 cups total liquid. Transfer to a small saucepan. In a small bowl, combine the cold water and the flour; stir into liquid in saucepan. Cook and stir until thickened and bubbly. Cook and stir for 1 minute more. Serve sauce with meat and vegetables. If desired, serve with hot cooked pasta.

Per serving: 286 cal., 11 g total fat (3 g sat. fat), 82 mg chol., 754 mg sodium, 8 g carb., 1 g fiber, 37 g pro.

Mexican-Stuffed Sweet Peppers

The colorful sweet peppers are perfect containers for the zesty filling of ground meat, cheese, and salsa.

Prep: 25 minutes
Cook: 6 to 7 hours (low) or 3 to 3½ hours (high)
Makes 4 servings

- 4 **medium green, red, and/or yellow sweet peppers**
- 1 **pound lean ground beef or ground pork**
- 1 **16-ounce jar black bean salsa or chunky salsa**
- 1½ **cups Monterey Jack cheese with jalapeño chile peppers or Monterey Jack cheese, shredded (6 ounces)**
- 1 **cup quick-cooking white rice**
- 1 **cup water**

1. Remove tops, membranes, and seeds from sweet peppers. For filling, in a large skillet, cook meat until brown; drain off fat. Stir salsa, 1 cup of the cheese, and the uncooked rice into meat in skillet. Spoon filling into peppers, mounding as needed.

2. Pour the water into a 4½- or 5-quart slow cooker. Arrange peppers, filling up, in the cooker.

3. Cover and cook on low-heat setting for 6 to 7 hours or on high-heat setting for 3 to 3½ hours. Transfer peppers to a serving platter. Top with remaining cheese.

Per serving: 513 cal., 24 g total fat (12 g sat. fat), 109 mg chol., 1,060 mg sodium, 38 g carb., 2 g fiber, 37 g pro.

Mediterranean Pot Roast

Fennel, tomatoes, olives, and Greek seasoning raise ordinary beef **brisket** to new flavor heights. Enjoy the **succulent** pot roast plain or spoon it over hot cooked **pasta or rice.**

Italian Beef Sandwiches

Brisket in Ale

The gravy for this fork-tender brisket is made from a tantalizing blend of beer, chili sauce, brown sugar, and seasonings.

Prep: 25 minutes
Cook: 10 to 12 hours (low) or 5 to 6 hours (high)
Makes 10 servings

1	3- to 4-pound fresh beef brisket
2	medium onions, thinly sliced and separated into rings
1	bay leaf
1	12-ounce can beer
¼	cup chili sauce
2	tablespoons packed brown sugar
½	teaspoon dried thyme, crushed
¼	teaspoon salt
¼	teaspoon ground black pepper
1	clove garlic, minced
2	tablespoons cornstarch
2	tablespoons cold water

1. Trim fat from meat. If necessary, cut meat to fit into a 3½- to 6-quart slow cooker. In the cooker, combine onions and bay leaf; top with meat. In a medium bowl, combine beer, chili sauce, brown sugar, thyme, salt, pepper, and garlic; pour over meat in cooker.

2. Cover and cook on low-heat setting for 10 to 12 hours or on high-heat setting for 5 to 6 hours.

3. Using a slotted spoon, transfer meat and onions to a platter; keep warm. Discard bay leaf. For gravy, skim fat from cooking liquid. Measure 2½ cups of the cooking liquid; discard remaining cooking liquid. In a medium saucepan, stir together cornstarch and the cold water; stir in the 2½ cups cooking liquid. Cook and stir until thickened and bubbly; cook and stir for 2 minutes more. Pass gravy with meat.

Per serving: 227 cal., 7 g total fat (2 g sat. fat), 78 mg chol., 242 mg sodium, 8 g carb., 1 g fiber, 30 g pro.

Italian Beef Sandwiches

Roasted red sweet peppers give these herbed beef sandwiches authentic flavor.

Prep: 15 minutes
Cook: 7 to 8 hours (low) or 3½ to 4 hours (high)
Makes 2 sandwiches

6	ounces beef flank steak
½	teaspoon dried oregano, crushed
	Dash crushed red pepper
1	clove garlic, minced
½	cup low-sodium tomato juice
¼	cup bottled roasted red sweet pepper strips (optional)
2	4-inch-long pieces French bread, split and toasted
¼	cup shredded provolone cheese (1 ounce)

1. Trim fat from meat. If necessary, cut meat to fit into a 1½-quart slow cooker. Place meat in cooker. Sprinkle with oregano, crushed red pepper, and garlic. Pour tomato juice over all.

2. Cover and cook on low-heat setting for 7 to 8 hours or on high-heat setting for 3½ to 4 hours. If no heat setting is available, cook for 6 to 7 hours.

3. Remove meat from cooker, reserving cooking juices. Using two forks, shred the meat. If desired, stir roasted pepper strips into shredded meat. Place shredded meat on bottoms of French bread pieces. Drizzle enough of the cooking juices over meat to moisten. Sprinkle shredded meat with cheese. Cover with tops of French bread pieces.

Per serving: 302 cal., 11 g total fat (5 g sat. fat), 44 mg chol., 442 mg sodium, 23 g carb., 2 g fiber, 26 g pro.

Beef in Red Wine Gravy

For a company-special meal, **team this tempting** wine-simmered beef dish with a crisp tossed salad, buttered peas, and crusty **bread.**

French Country Soup

Crusty pieces of French bread are perfect for soaking up the wonderful rosemary-seasoned broth in this bean-and-beef combo.

Prep: 20 minutes
Stand: 1 hour
Cook: 8 to 10 hours (low) or 4 to 5 hours (high)
Makes 6 servings

8	ounces dry navy, Great Northern, or white kidney (cannellini) beans
6	cups water
1	pound beef or lamb stew meat, cut into 1-inch cubes
4	cups reduced-sodium chicken broth
2	medium carrots, cut into 1-inch pieces
2	stalks celery, cut into 1-inch pieces
1	large onion, cut into wedges
1	cup dry white wine
6	cloves garlic, minced
3	bay leaves
1½	teaspoons dried rosemary, crushed
½	teaspoon salt
¼	teaspoon ground black pepper

1. Rinse and drain beans. In a 4-quart Dutch oven, combine beans and the water. Bring to boiling; reduce heat. Simmer for 10 minutes. Remove from heat. Cover and let stand for 1 hour.

2. Drain beans in colander; rinse beans. In a 3½- to 6-quart slow cooker, combine beans, meat, broth, carrots, celery, onion, wine, garlic, bay leaves, rosemary, salt, and pepper.

3. Cover and cook on low-heat setting for 8 to 10 hours or on high-heat setting for 4 to 5 hours. Discard bay leaves.

Per serving: 315 cal., 4 g total fat (1 g sat. fat), 45 mg chol., 694 mg sodium, 37 g carb., 12 g fiber, 28 g pro.

Beef in Red Wine Gravy

This hearty stew is the perfect way to use red wine left over from a party. If you buy a new bottle of wine, choose the same quality you would drink.

Prep: 15 minutes
Cook: 10 to 12 hours (low) or 5 to 6 hours (high)
Makes 6 servings

1½	pounds beef stew meat, cut into 1-inch cubes
2	medium onions, cut up
2	beef bouillon cubes or 1 envelope (½ of 2-ounce package) onion soup mix
3	tablespoons cornstarch
	Salt
	Ground black pepper
1½	cups dry red wine
	Hot cooked noodles (optional)

1. In a 3½- or 4-quart slow cooker, combine meat and onions. Add bouillon cubes or dry onion soup mix. Sprinkle cornstarch, salt, and pepper over meat and onions. Pour red wine over mixture in cooker.

2. Cover and cook on low-heat setting for 10 to 12 hours or on high-heat setting for 5 to 6 hours.

3. If desired, serve over hot cooked noodles.

Per serving: 211 cal., 4 g total fat (1 g sat. fat), 67 mg chol., 430 mg sodium, 8 g carb., 0 g fiber, 24 g pro.

Thaw Meat First

Don't put frozen meat or poultry directly into a slow cooker. If the meat thaws as it cooks, the mixture will be in a temperature zone (40°F to 140°F) where bacteria thrive for too long. Thaw frozen meat or poultry completely in the refrigerator before adding it to the slow cooker.

Beef Fajitas

Prep: 25 minutes
Cook: 7 to 8 hours (low) or 3½ to 4 hours (high)
Makes 8 servings

- 1 **large onion, cut into thin wedges**
- 2 **pounds boneless beef sirloin steak**
- 1 **teaspoon ground cumin**
- 1 **teaspoon ground coriander**
- ½ **teaspoon salt**
- ½ **teaspoon ground black pepper**
- 2 **medium red or green sweet peppers, cut into thin, bite-size strips**
- ¼ **cup beef broth**
- 8 **7- to 8-inch whole wheat or plain flour tortillas**
- 1 **cup shredded carrot**
- 1 **cup coarsely shredded lettuce**
  Salsa, sour cream, and guacamole

1. Place onion in a 3½- or 4-quart slow cooker. Trim fat from meat. Sprinkle one side of the meat with cumin, coriander, salt, and black pepper; rub in with your fingers. Cut meat across the grain into thin, bite-size strips. Add meat strips to cooker. Top with sweet pepper. Pour broth over all.

2. Cover and cook on low-heat setting for 7 to 8 hours or on high-heat setting for 3½ to 4 hours.

3. To serve, use a slotted spoon to spoon meat-vegetable mixture onto tortillas. Top each serving with carrot and lettuce. Fold tortillas over. Serve with salsa, sour cream, and guacamole.

Per serving: 327 cal., 10 g total fat (3 g sat. fat), 70 mg chol., 642 mg sodium, 22 g carb., 12 g fiber, 33 g pro.

Mediterranean Meat Loaf

Feta cheese, oregano, and dried tomatoes load this meat loaf with Mediterranean flavor.
Prep: 20 minutes
Cook: 7 to 8 hours (low) or 3½ to 4 hours (high)
Makes 4 to 6 servings

- 1 **egg**
- 2 **tablespoons milk**
- ½ **cup fine dry bread crumbs**
- ½ **teaspoon salt**
- ½ **teaspoon dried oregano, crushed**
- ¼ **teaspoon ground black pepper**
- 2 **cloves garlic, minced**
- 1½ **pounds lean ground beef**
- ½ **cup crumbled feta cheese (2 ounces)**
- ¼ **cup oil-packed dried tomatoes, drained and snipped**
- 3 **tablespoons bottled pizza or pasta sauce**

1. In a medium bowl, combine egg and milk; beat with a fork. Stir in bread crumbs, salt, oregano, pepper, and garlic. Add meat, feta cheese, and dried tomatoes; mix well. Shape meat mixture into a 5-inch round loaf.

2. Tear off an 18-inch square piece of heavy foil. Cut into thirds. Fold each piece into thirds lengthwise. Crisscross strips and place meat loaf in center of foil strips. Bringing up strips, transfer loaf and foil to a 3½- or 4-quart slow cooker (leave foil strips under loaf). Press loaf away from side of cooker. Fold strips down, leaving loaf exposed. Spread pizza sauce over loaf.

3. Cover and cook on low-heat setting for 7 to 8 hours or on high-heat setting for 3½ to 4 hours.

4. Using foil strips, carefully lift meat loaf from cooker. Discard foil strips.

Per serving: 396 cal., 22 g total fat (9 g sat. fat), 173 mg chol., 873 mg sodium, 12 g carb., 1 g fiber, 36 g pro.

Colorful toppings, including zesty **guacamole,** velvety **sour cream,** and tongue-tingling **salsa,** boost the flavor of these **Tex-Mex** meat-and-veggie bundles.

Beef Fajitas

Beef Lo Mein

Beef Lo Mein

Thanks to ready-made stir-fry sauce and your slow cooker, this Asian classic has never been easier!

Prep: 25 minutes
Cook: 7 to 9 hours (low) or 3½ to 4½ hours (high), plus 30 minutes on high
Makes 8 servings

2	pounds boneless beef sirloin steak, cut 1 inch thick
1	tablespoon cooking oil
1	large onion, sliced
1	8-ounce can sliced water chestnuts, drained
1	4½-ounce jar (drained weight) whole mushrooms, drained
1	12.1-ounce jar stir-fry sauce
1	tablespoon quick-cooking tapioca
1	16-ounce package loose-pack frozen broccoli, cauliflower, and carrots
⅓	cup cashews
12	ounces dried lo mein noodles

1. Trim fat from meat. Cut meat into 1-inch pieces. In a large skillet, brown meat, half at a time, in hot oil. Drain off fat. Set aside.

2. Place onion in a 3½- or 4-quart slow cooker. Add meat, water chestnuts, and mushrooms. In a small bowl, stir together stir-fry sauce and tapioca. Pour over mixture in cooker.

3. Cover and cook on low-heat setting for 7 to 9 hours or on high-heat setting for 3½ to 4½ hours.

4. If using low-heat setting, turn to high-heat setting. Stir in frozen vegetables. Cover and cook for 30 to 40 minutes more or until vegetables are crisp-tender. Stir in cashews. Meanwhile, cook lo mein noodles according to package directions; drain. Serve meat mixture over lo mein noodles.

Per serving: 447 cal., 11 g total fat (2 g sat. fat), 95 mg chol., 995 mg sodium, 52 g carb., 4 g fiber, 35 g pro.

North African Beef Stew

Cumin, cayenne, and cinnamon give this beef-and-fruit stew its interesting North African flavor.

Prep: 20 minutes
Cook: 7½ to 8½ hours (low), plus 30 minutes, or 3½ to 4 hours (high), plus 30 minutes
Makes 6 servings

1½	pounds lean beef stew meat
2	medium sweet potatoes, peeled, halved lengthwise, and cut into ½-inch-thick slices
1	medium onion, cut into wedges
1	cup water
1	teaspoon instant beef bouillon granules
¾	teaspoon ground cumin
¼	teaspoon cayenne pepper
⅛	teaspoon ground cinnamon
4	cloves garlic, minced
1	14½-ounce can diced tomatoes, undrained
½	cup dried apricots or pitted dried plums (prunes), quartered
	Hot cooked couscous (optional)
¼	cup chopped peanuts

1. Cut meat into 1-inch pieces. In a 3½- or 4-quart slow cooker, combine meat, sweet potatoes, and onion. Stir in the water, bouillon granules, cumin, cayenne pepper, cinnamon, and garlic.

2. Cover and cook on low-heat setting for 7½ to 8½ hours or on high-heat setting for 3½ to 4 hours.

3. Stir in undrained tomatoes and dried apricots. Cover and cook for 30 minutes more. If desired, serve meat mixture over hot cooked couscous. Sprinkle individual servings with peanuts.

Per serving: 274 cal., 7 g total fat (2 g sat. fat), 67 mg chol., 373 mg sodium, 24 g carb., 4 g fiber, 27 g pro.

Moroccan-Style Short Ribs

Couscous flecked with almonds and olives provides a **soothing counterpoint** to these spicy beef **short ribs,** garbanzo beans, and **vegetables.**

Moroccan-Style Short Ribs

Prep: 30 minutes
Cook: 9 to 10 hours (low) or 4½ to 5 hours (high)
Makes 8 servings

- 1 **tablespoon dried thyme, crushed**
- 1 **teaspoon salt**
- 1 **teaspoon ground ginger**
- 1 **teaspoon ground black pepper**
- ½ **teaspoon ground cinnamon**
- 3½ **pounds beef short ribs**
- 2 **tablespoons olive oil**
- 3 **cups beef broth**
- 1 **16-ounce can garbanzo beans (chickpeas), rinsed and drained**
- 1 **14½-ounce can diced tomatoes, undrained**
- 1 **large onion, cut into thin wedges**
- 1 **medium fennel bulb, trimmed and cut into thin wedges**
- 1 **cup chopped carrot**
- 4 **cloves garlic, minced**
- 1 **10-ounce package quick-cooking couscous**
- ½ **cup sliced almonds, toasted**
- ½ **cup pitted kalamata olives, halved**

1. In a small bowl, combine thyme, salt, ginger, pepper, and cinnamon. Sprinkle evenly over short ribs; rub in with your fingers. In a large skillet, brown short ribs, half at a time, in hot oil over medium-high heat. Drain off fat. In a 6- to 7-quart slow cooker, combine broth, beans, undrained tomatoes, onion, fennel, carrot, and garlic; top with short ribs.

2. Cover and cook on low-heat setting for 9 to 10 hours or on high-heat setting for 4½ to 5 hours. Using a slotted spoon, transfer ribs and vegetables to a serving dish. If desired, moisten with cooking liquid. Meanwhile, prepare couscous according to package directions. Stir in almonds and olives. Serve with short ribs and vegetables.

Per serving: 441 cal., 17 g total fat (4 g sat. fat), 46 mg chol., 1,064 mg sodium, 45 g carb., 6 g fiber, 26 g pro.

Ginger and Orange-Glazed Short Ribs

When it comes to a down-to-earth comfort meal, it's hard to beat beef short ribs. Here, the ribs get special treatment with five-spice powder and other Asian flavorings.

Prep: 20 minutes
Cook: 11 to 12 hours (low) or 5½ to 6 hours (high)
Makes 4 to 6 servings

- 3 **pounds beef short ribs**
- 1 **large red onion, cut into wedges**
- 1 **cup orange marmalade**
- ⅓ **cup water**
- 2 **tablespoons rice vinegar**
- 1 **tablespoon soy sauce**
- 2 **teaspoons five-spice powder**
- 2 **teaspoons grated fresh ginger**
- ½ **to 1½ teaspoons chile oil**
- 2 **cloves garlic, minced**

1. Trim fat from short ribs. Set short ribs aside. Place red onion in a 3½- to 5-quart slow cooker. Add short ribs. In a medium bowl, combine orange marmalade, the water, rice vinegar, soy sauce, five-spice powder, ginger, chile oil, and garlic. Reserve ⅔ cup of the marmalade mixture for sauce; cover and chill. Pour the remaining marmalade mixture over ribs and onion in cooker.

2. Cover and cook on low-heat setting for 11 to 12 hours or on high-heat setting for 5½ to 6 hours.

3. For sauce, in a small saucepan, heat reserved marmalade mixture until boiling; reduce heat. Boil gently, uncovered, for 5 minutes. Remove short ribs and onion from cooker; discard cooking liquid. Serve short ribs and onion with sauce.

Per serving: 452 cal., 12 g total fat (5 g sat. fat), 64 mg chol., 385 mg sodium, 58 g carb., 1 g fiber, 29 g pro.

Cranberry-Chipotle Beef

Looking for a slow-cooked roast that serves just two? This fiery chipotle-seasoned chuck roast is a delicious possibility.

Prep: 10 minutes
Cook: 6 to 8 hours (low) or 3 to 4 hours (high)
Makes 2 servings

1	small onion, cut into thin wedges
12	ounces beef chuck roast
⅛	teaspoon salt
⅛	teaspoon ground black pepper
1	clove garlic, minced
½	of a 16-ounce can (about ¾ cup) whole cranberry sauce
½	to 1 teaspoon finely chopped canned chipotle chile peppers in adobo sauce (see tip, page 77)
1	cup instant brown rice
	Fresh jalapeño chile peppers, halved (optional) (see tip, page 77)

1. Place onion in a 1½-quart slow cooker. If necessary, cut meat to fit into cooker; add to cooker. Sprinkle with salt, black pepper, and garlic. Combine cranberry sauce and chipotle peppers. Pour over all.

2. Cover and cook on low-heat setting for 6 to 8 hours or on high-heat setting for 3 to 4 hours. If no heat setting is available, cook for 4½ to 5½ hours.

3. To serve, cook rice according to package directions, except omit salt and butter. Serve meat mixture with rice. If desired, garnish with jalapeño peppers.

Per serving: 506 cal., 7 g total fat (2 g sat. fat), 101 mg chol., 296 mg sodium, 71 g carb., 4 g fiber, 40 g pro.

Rich Beef and Barley Soup

Vary the character of this hearty beef soup by the type of spaghetti sauce you choose. One time try a sauce with lots garlic or mushrooms and another time use an herb-seasoned sauce.

Prep: 30 minutes
Cook: 9 to 10 hours (low) or 4½ to 5 hours (high)
Makes 6 to 8 servings

1½	pounds beef stew meat
1	tablespoon cooking oil
1	cup thinly sliced carrot
1	cup sliced celery
1	medium onion, thinly sliced
½	cup coarsely chopped green sweet pepper
4	cups beef broth
1	14½-ounce can tomatoes, undrained, cut up
1	cup purchased spaghetti sauce
⅔	cup pearl barley
1½	teaspoons dried basil, crushed
½	teaspoon salt
¼	teaspoon ground black pepper
¼	cup snipped fresh parsley

1. Cut meat into 1-inch pieces. In a large skillet, brown meat, half at a time, in hot oil. Drain well.

2. Meanwhile, in a 3½- to 6-quart slow cooker, combine carrot, celery, onion, and sweet pepper. Add broth, undrained tomatoes, spaghetti sauce, barley, basil, salt, and pepper. Stir in browned meat.

3. Cover and cook on low-heat setting for 9 to 10 hours or on high-heat setting for 4½ to 5 hours. Skim off fat. Stir in parsley.

Per serving: 408 cal., 19 g total fat (7 g sat. fat), 72 mg chol., 998 mg sodium, 30 g carb., 6 g fiber, 29 g pro.

Cranberry-Chipotle Beef

Mixed dried fruit, **cranberries,** orange juice, molasses, cinnamon, and nutmeg **dress up** plain-Jane **corned beef** with lively new flavor.

Orange-Spiced Corned Beef with Dried Fruit

Smoky Barbecued Beef Brisket

If you like, pile this zesty beef into buns or hard rolls and spoon on some creamy coleslaw as a topper.

Prep: 15 minutes
Cook: 10 to 11 hours (low) or 5 to 5½ hours (high)
Makes 6 to 8 servings

- 1 **2- to 3-pound fresh beef brisket**
- 1 **teaspoon chili powder**
- ½ **teaspoon garlic powder**
- ¼ **teaspoon celery seeds**
- ⅛ **teaspoon ground black pepper**
- ½ **cup ketchup**
- ½ **cup chili sauce**
- ¼ **cup packed brown sugar**
- 2 **tablespoons vinegar**
- 2 **tablespoons Worcestershire sauce**
- 1½ **teaspoons liquid smoke**
- ½ **teaspoon dry mustard**
- ⅓ **cup cold water**
- 3 **tablespoons all-purpose flour**

1. Trim fat from meat. Cut meat to fit into a 3½- or 4-quart slow cooker. In a small bowl, combine chili powder, garlic powder, celery seeds, and pepper. Sprinkle chili powder mixture evenly over meat; rub in with your fingers. Place meat in the slow cooker.

2. In a medium bowl, combine ketchup, chili sauce, brown sugar, vinegar, Worcestershire sauce, liquid smoke, and dry mustard. Pour over meat in cooker.

3. Cover and cook on low-heat setting for 10 to 11 hours or on high-heat setting for 5 to 5½ hours.

4. Remove meat from cooker, reserving cooking juices. Skim fat off cooking juices; measure 2½ cups of the cooking juices. For sauce, in a medium saucepan, stir the cold water into flour; add the 2½ cups cooking juices. Cook and stir until thickened and bubbly; cook and stir for 1 minute more.

Cutting across the grain, cut the meat into thin slices. Serve sauce with meat.

Per serving: 305 cal., 8 g total fat (2 g sat. fat), 87 mg chol., 681 mg sodium, 24 g carb., 2 g fiber, 34 g pro.

Orange-Spiced Corned Beef with Dried Fruit

Prep: 15 minutes
Cook: 8 to 10 hours (low) or 4 to 5 hours (high)
Makes 6 servings

- 1 **2½- to 3-pound corned beef brisket**
- 1 **7-ounce package mixed dried fruit**
- ½ **cup dried cranberries**
- 2 **tablespoons quick-cooking tapioca**
- ½ **cup orange juice**
- ½ **cup water**
- 1 **tablespoon mild-flavored molasses**
- ¼ **teaspoon ground cinnamon**
- ⅛ **teaspoon ground nutmeg**

1. Trim fat from meat. If necessary, cut meat to fit into a 3½- or 4-quart slow cooker. If a seasoning packet is present, discard it. Place meat in the cooker.

2. Cut any large pieces of mixed dried fruit into quarters. Sprinkle mixed dried fruit, dried cranberries, and tapioca over meat in cooker. In a small bowl, combine orange juice, the water, molasses, cinnamon, and nutmeg. Pour over mixture in cooker.

3. Cover and cook on low-heat setting for 8 to 10 hours or on high-heat setting for 4 to 5 hours.

4. Remove meat from cooker. Thinly slice meat across the grain. Arrange meat slices on a serving platter. Spoon fruit mixture over meat.

Per serving: 617 cal., 36 g total fat (12 g sat. fat), 185 mg chol., 2,151 mg sodium, 38 g carb., 2 g fiber, 35 g pro.

Polenta with Ground Beef Ragoût

Ground pork or lamb would be equally tasty in this hearty stew.

Prep: 25 minutes
Cook: 7 to 9 hours (low) or 3½ to 4½ hours (high), plus 30 minutes on high
Makes 6 servings

1	pound lean ground beef
1	14½-ounce can Italian-style stewed tomatoes, undrained
3	medium carrots, cut into ½-inch-thick slices
2	medium onions, cut into thin wedges
1	large red sweet pepper, cut into 1-inch pieces
½	cup beef broth
¼	teaspoon salt
¼	teaspoon ground black pepper
6	cloves garlic, minced
1	medium zucchini, halved lengthwise and cut into ¼-inch-thick slices
1	16-ounce tube refrigerated cooked polenta
6	tablespoons purchased pesto or olive tapenade
	Fresh basil sprigs (optional)

1. In a large skillet, cook meat until brown. Drain off fat. Transfer meat to a 3½- or 4-quart slow cooker. Stir in undrained tomatoes, carrots, onions, sweet pepper, broth, salt, black pepper, and garlic.

2. Cover and cook on low-heat setting for 7 to 9 hours or on high-heat setting for 3½ to 4½ hours.

3. If using low-heat setting, turn to high-heat setting. Stir in zucchini. Cover and cook about 30 minutes more or until zucchini is crisp-tender.

4. Meanwhile, prepare polenta according to package directions. Serve meat mixture over polenta. Top individual servings with pesto. If desired, garnish with basil sprigs.

Per serving: 388 cal., 20 g total fat (4 g sat. fat), 50 mg chol., 773 mg sodium, 30 g carb., 5 g fiber, 20 g pro.

Beef Brisket with Potatoes

If you like meat and potatoes, you'll love this brisket with two types of potatoes. The sauce is a tongue-tingling mix of hoisin sauce, salsa, and garlic.

Prep: 20 minutes
Cook: 10 hours (low) or 5 to 5½ hours (high)
Makes 8 servings

1	pound baking potatoes, peeled and cut into 1-inch cubes
1	pound sweet potatoes, peeled and cut into 1-inch cubes
1	3- to 3½-pound fresh beef brisket, fat trimmed
½	cup bottled hoisin sauce
½	cup purchased salsa
2	tablespoons quick-cooking tapioca
2	cloves garlic, minced

1. In a 5- to 6-quart slow cooker, combine baking potatoes and sweet potatoes. Top with meat. In a small bowl, combine hoisin sauce, salsa, tapioca, and garlic. Pour salsa mixture over meat in cooker; spread evenly.

2. Cover and cook on low-heat setting for 10 hours or on high-heat setting for 5 to 5½ hours.

3. Transfer meat from cooker to a cutting board. Cut meat across the grain into slices. Serve cooking liquid and potatoes over beef.

Per serving: 344 cal., 11 g total fat (3 g sat. fat), 103 mg chol., 382 mg sodium, 22 g carb., 2 g fiber, 38 g pro.

Sliced polenta on the bottom and a spoonful of **pesto or olive tapenade** on top add a gourmet twist to this slow-simmered **beef.**

Polenta with Ground Beef Ragoût

Beef-Vegetable Soup

Beef-Vegetable Soup

On a super-busy day, start this soup simmering before leaving home, and it will be ready to serve when dinnertime rolls around.

Prep: 25 minutes
Cook: 8 to 10 hours (low) or 4 to 5 hours (high)
Makes 4 or 5 servings

1	**pound boneless beef chuck roast, cut into 1-inch pieces**
1	**tablespoon cooking oil**
2	**14½-ounce cans diced tomatoes, undrained**
1	**cup water**
3	**medium carrots, sliced**
2	**small potatoes, peeled if desired, cut into ½-inch cubes**
1	**cup chopped onion**
1	**teaspoon salt**
½	**teaspoon dried thyme, crushed**
½	**cup loose-pack frozen peas, thawed**

1. In a large skillet, brown meat in hot oil over medium-high heat.

2. Transfer meat to a 3½- to 4½-quart slow cooker. Add undrained tomatoes, the water, carrots, potatoes, onion, salt, and thyme to cooker.

3. Cover and cook on low-heat setting for 8 to 10 hours or on high-heat setting for 4 or 5 hours. Stir in peas.

Per serving: 335 cal., 8 g total fat (2 g sat. fat), 67 mg chol., 1,054 mg sodium, 35 g carb., 5 g fiber, 29 g pro.

Gingered Beef and Vegetables

Saucy Pot Roast with Noodles

Saucy Pot Roast with Noodles

Prep: 25 minutes
Cook: 10 to 12 hours (low) or 4 to 5 hours (high)
Makes 6 to 8 servings

1	**2- to 2½-pound beef chuck pot roast**
1	**tablespoon cooking oil**
2	**medium carrots, sliced**
2	**stalks celery, sliced**
1	**medium onion, sliced**
2	**cloves garlic, minced**
1	**tablespoon quick-cooking tapioca**
1	**14½-ounce can Italian-style stewed tomatoes, undrained**
1	**6-ounce can Italian-style tomato paste**
1	**tablespoon packed brown sugar**
½	**teaspoon salt**
¼	**teaspoon ground black pepper**
1	**bay leaf**
	Hot cooked noodles
	Celery leaves (optional)

1. Trim fat from meat. If necessary, cut meat to fit into a 3½- or 4-quart slow cooker. In a large skillet, brown meat on all sides in hot oil.

2. In the cooker, combine carrots, celery, onion, and garlic. Sprinkle tapioca over vegetables. Arrange meat to cover vegetables.

3. In a medium bowl, combine undrained tomatoes, tomato paste, brown sugar, salt, pepper, and bay leaf; pour over the roast in cooker.

4. Cover and cook on low-heat setting for 10 to 12 hours or on high-setting for 4 to 5 hours.

5. Discard bay leaf. Skim off fat. Slice meat. Serve with noodles. If desired, garnish with celery leaves.

Per serving: 569 cal., 27 g total fat (10 g sat. fat), 127 mg chol., 693 mg sodium, 48 g carb., 4 g fiber, 32 g pro.

Barbecue Pork Ribs

No need to fire up the grill for these spunky barbecued ribs—they just simmer away in your slow cooker. If you have any leftovers, shred the meat to make sandwiches.

Prep: 25 minutes
Cook: 10 to 12 hours (low) or 5 to 6 hours (high)
Makes 4 to 6 servings

- 3 to 3½ pounds pork country-style ribs
- 1 cup ketchup
- ½ cup finely chopped onion
- ¼ cup packed brown sugar
- 1 tablespoon Worcestershire sauce
- ½ teaspoon chili powder
- ½ teaspoon liquid smoke
- ¼ teaspoon garlic powder
- ¼ teaspoon bottled hot pepper sauce

1. Place ribs in a 3½- or 4-quart slow cooker. In a small bowl, combine ketchup, onion, brown sugar, Worcestershire sauce, chili powder, liquid smoke, garlic powder, and hot pepper sauce. Pour over ribs in cooker, turning ribs to coat.

2. Cover and cook on low-heat setting for 10 to 12 hours or on high-heat setting for 5 to 6 hours.

3. Transfer ribs to a platter; cover to keep warm. Skim fat from surface of sauce; pour sauce into a medium saucepan. Bring sauce to boiling; reduce heat slightly. Boil gently, uncovered, for 5 to 7 minutes or until thickened to desired consistency (should make about 1 cup). Pass sauce with ribs.

Per serving: 419 cal., 15 g total fat (5 g sat. fat), 121 mg chol., 891 mg sodium, 33 g carb., 2 g fiber, 38 g pro.

Black Bean and Kielbasa Soup

Round out this hearty sausage-and-bean combo with corn bread sticks or muffins.

Prep: 15 minutes
Cook: 6 to 8 hours (low) or 3 to 4 hours (high)
Makes 6 servings

- 2 19-ounce cans ready-to-serve black bean soup
- 1 14½-ounce can diced tomatoes with garlic and onion, undrained
- 1 pound cooked, smoked Polish sausage, halved lengthwise and cut into ½-inch-thick slices
- 1 cup loose-pack frozen whole kernel corn

1. In a 3½- to 4½-quart slow cooker, stir together black bean soup, undrained tomatoes, sausage, and corn.

2. Cover and cook on low-heat setting for 6 to 8 hours or on high-heat setting for 3 to 4 hours.

Per serving: 425 cal., 24 g total fat (11 g sat. fat), 55 mg chol., 1,487 mg sodium, 34 g carb., 8 g fiber, 17 g pro.

Chop, Chop

Here's a foolproof way to chop an onion. Peel the onion and halve it from top to root end. Place one half, flat side down, on a cutting board. Cut horizontal slices across the half. Then, holding the slices together, cut vertical slices. Repeat with the second onion half.

Tomato-Sauced Pork Chops

Ginger Pork and Dried Plums

This pork roast owes its pleasant sweetness to apples and dried plums and its fabulous flavor to an intriguing mix of ginger, cinnamon, pepper, and cloves.

Prep: 20 minutes
Cook: 7 to 8 hours (low) or 3½ to 4 hours (high)
Makes 6 servings

1	**2-pound boneless pork shoulder roast**
3	**tablespoons quick-cooking tapioca**
2	**medium cooking apples, peeled, cored, and cut into ½-inch-thick slices**
4	**medium carrots, bias-sliced into ½-inch-thick pieces**
1	**medium onion, cut into 1-inch chunks**
1	**cup pitted dried plums (prunes), quartered**
1	**cup chicken broth**
¾	**cup apple juice or apple cider**
1	**tablespoon lemon juice**
1	**teaspoon ground ginger**
¼	**teaspoon ground cinnamon**
¼	**teaspoon ground black pepper**
⅛	**teaspoon ground cloves**
	Hot cooked couscous or noodles

1. Trim fat from meat. Cut meat into 1-inch cubes. Place meat in a 3½- or 4-quart slow cooker. Sprinkle tapioca over meat. Add apples, carrots, onion, dried plums, broth, apple juice, lemon juice, ginger, cinnamon, pepper, and cloves. Stir to combine.

2. Cover and cook on low-heat setting for 7 to 8 hours or on high-heat setting for 3½ to 4 hours.

3. Serve with hot cooked couscous.

Per serving: 505 cal., 12 g total fat (4 g sat. fat), 102 mg chol., 297 mg sodium, 76 g carb., 7 g fiber, 37 g pro.

Tomato-Sauced Pork Chops

Toss some hot cooked pasta with a little olive oil and snipped fresh basil to serve alongside these Italian-inspired chops.

Prep: 15 minutes
Cook: 7 to 8 hours (low) or 3½ to 4 hours (high)
Makes 6 servings

6	**boneless pork loin chops, cut ¾ inch thick**
1	**tablespoon cooking oil**
1	**envelope (½ of a 2-ounce package) onion soup mix**
1	**15-ounce can Great Northern or small white beans, rinsed and drained**
1	**14½-ounce can diced tomatoes with basil, oregano, and garlic, undrained**
2	**tablespoons dry red wine or water**

1. Trim fat from chops. In a 12-inch skillet, brown chops in hot oil. Drain off fat. Transfer chops to a 3½- or 4-quart slow cooker. Sprinkle chops with dry onion soup mix. Pour beans and undrained tomatoes over chops in cooker.

2. Cover and cook on low-heat setting for 7 to 8 hours or on high-heat setting for 3½ to 4 hours.

3. Transfer chops to a serving platter. Stir wine into bean mixture. Using a slotted spoon, spoon beans and tomatoes over chops; discard cooking liquid.

Per serving: 381 cal., 11 g total fat (3 g sat. fat), 93 mg chol., 594 mg sodium, 24 g carb., 4 g fiber, 44 g pro.

Peppery Pork Sandwiches

For a milder sandwich, use regular paprika instead of the hot version.

Prep: 25 minutes
Cook: 10 to 12 hours (low) or 5 to 6 hours (high)
Makes 8 or 9 sandwiches

 1 **large onion**
 1 **2- to 2½-pound boneless pork shoulder roast**
 1 **tablespoon hot paprika**
 2 **14½-ounce cans diced tomatoes, undrained**
 1 **4-ounce can diced green chile peppers, undrained**
 2 **teaspoons dried oregano, crushed**
 ½ **to 1 teaspoon ground black pepper**
 ¼ **teaspoon salt**
 8 **or 9 individual French-style rolls, split and toasted**

1. Cut onion lengthwise into quarters; thinly slice quarters. Arrange onion slices in bottom of a 4- to 5-quart slow cooker. Trim fat from meat. Sprinkle meat evenly with paprika. Place meat on top of onion. In a medium bowl, combine undrained tomatoes, chile peppers, oregano, black pepper, and salt; pour over meat in cooker.

2. Cover and cook on low-heat setting for 10 to 12 hours or on high-heat setting for 5 to 6 hours.

3. Transfer meat to cutting board, reserving cooking liquid and tomato mixture. Using two forks, pull meat into shreds and place in a large bowl, discarding total fat. Using a slotted spoon, remove tomatoes and onions from cooking liquid; add to shredded meat. Add enough of the cooking liquid to moisten. Spoon meat mixture onto rolls.

Per serving: 512 cal., 12 g total fat (3 g sat. fat), 73 mg chol., 1,066 mg sodium, 65 g carb., 5 g fiber, 33 g pro.

Peach-Glazed Pork Roast with Corn Bread Stuffing

Fruit-studded stuffing topped with a peach-glazed roast—now that's a meal to savor!

Prep: 25 minutes
Cook: 5 to 6 hours (low) or 2½ to 3 hours (high)
Makes 8 servings

    Nonstick cooking spray
 1 **2- to 2½-pound boneless pork top loin roast (single loin)**
    Salt
    Ground black pepper
 1 **tablespoon cooking oil**
 4 **cups corn bread stuffing mix**
 ¾ **cup reduced-sodium chicken broth**
 ½ **cup mixed dried fruit bits**
 ¼ **cup chopped onion**
 ½ **cup peach spreadable fruit**
 1 **teaspoon finely shredded lemon peel**
 ¼ **teaspoon ground cinnamon**

1. Lightly coat a 3½- or 4-quart slow cooker with cooking spray. Trim fat from meat. If necessary, cut meat to fit into cooker. Sprinkle meat with salt and pepper. In a large skillet, brown meat on all sides in hot oil. Drain off fat. Set aside.

2. In a large bowl, toss together stuffing mix, broth, dried fruit, and onion. Place stuffing mixture in prepared cooker. Add meat. In a small bowl, stir together peach spreadable fruit, lemon peel, and cinnamon. Spread over meat in cooker.

3. Cover and cook on low-heat setting for 5 to 6 hours or on high-heat setting for 2½ to 3 hours.

4. Remove meat from cooker. Slice meat. Stir stuffing; serve with meat.

Per serving: 408 cal., 9 g total fat (2 g sat. fat), 67 mg chol., 639 mg sodium, 52 g carb., 0 g fiber, 29 g pro.

Peppery Pork Sandwiches

Shredded **pork sandwiches** take on a
delicious new **attitude** when green chile peppers,
tomatoes, oregano, and **hot paprika** season
the **meat.**

Italian Pork with Mashed Sweet Potatoes

Texas Two-Step Stew

Serve this wake-your-taste buds stew with warm flour tortillas, cool sour cream, and tangy lime wedges.

Prep: 20 minutes
Cook: 4 to 6 hours (low), plus 1 hour, or 2 to 3 hours (high), plus 45 minutes
Makes 6 servings

- 8 ounces uncooked chorizo sausage (remove casings if present)
- 1 medium onion, chopped
- 1 15-ounce can Mexican-style or Tex-Mex-style chili beans, undrained
- 1 15-ounce can hominy or one 11-ounce can whole kernel corn with sweet peppers, drained
- 1 6-ounce package regular Spanish-style rice mix
- 6 cups water

1. In a medium skillet, cook sausage and onion over medium heat until sausage is brown. Drain off fat. Transfer sausage mixture to a 3½- or 4-quart slow cooker. Stir in undrained chili beans, hominy, and, if present, the seasoning packet contents from the rice mix (set aside remaining rice mix). Pour the water over all. Cover and cook on low-heat setting for 4 to 6 hours or on high-heat setting for 2 to 3 hours.

2. Stir in remaining rice mix. Cover and cook on low-heat setting for 1 hour more or on high-heat setting for 45 minutes more.

Per serving: 383 cal., 16 g total fat (6 g sat. fat), 33 mg chol., 1,385 mg sodium, 44 g carb., 6 g fiber, 16 g pro.

Italian Pork with Mashed Sweet Potatoes

A fennel seed rub coats this pork with extraordinary licoricelike flavor while the golden-orange potatoes add just the right amount of sweetness.

Prep: 20 minutes
Cook: 8 to 10 hours (low) or 4 to 5 hours (high)
Makes 4 servings

- 1 teaspoon fennel seeds, crushed
- ½ teaspoon dried oregano, crushed
- ½ teaspoon garlic powder
- ½ teaspoon paprika
- ¼ teaspoon salt
- ¼ teaspoon ground black pepper
- 1 1½- to 2-pound boneless pork shoulder roast
- 1 pound sweet potatoes, peeled and cut into 1-inch pieces
- 1 cup chicken broth

1. In a small bowl, combine fennel seeds, oregano, garlic powder, paprika, salt, and pepper. Trim fat from meat. Sprinkle fennel seed mixture evenly over meat; rub in with your fingers. If necessary, cut meat to fit into a 3½- or 4-quart slow cooker. Set aside.

2. Place sweet potatoes in cooker. Add meat. Pour broth over mixture in cooker.

3. Cover and cook on low-heat setting for 8 to 10 hours or on high-heat setting for 4 to 5 hours.

4. Remove meat from cooker, reserving cooking juices. Slice meat. Using a slotted spoon, transfer sweet potatoes to a medium bowl. Use a potato masher to mash sweet potatoes, adding some of the cooking juices, if necessary, to moisten. Serve meat with mashed sweet potatoes.

Per serving: 356 cal., 14 g total fat (5 g sat. fat), 115 mg chol., 525 mg sodium, 21 g carb., 3 g fiber, 35 g pro.

Smoked Sausage-Lentil Soup

Prep: 25 minutes
Cook: 6 to 7 hours (low) or 3 to 3½ hours (high)
Makes 6 servings

1	small fennel bulb
6	cups water
6	ounces smoked sausage, cut into ½-inch pieces
1¼	cups dry brown lentils, rinsed and drained
2	carrots, chopped
1	medium onion, chopped
4	cloves garlic, minced
1	teaspoon kosher or sea salt or ¾ teaspoon regular salt
¼	teaspoon freshly ground black pepper
2	tablespoons red wine vinegar
	Kosher salt, sea salt, or regular salt
	Freshly ground black pepper

1. Remove fennel tops and reserve for garnish. Chop enough of the fennel bulb to equal 1 cup.

2. In a 3½- to 5-quart slow cooker, combine fennel, the water, sausage, lentils, carrots, onion, garlic, the salt, and the ¼ teaspoon pepper.

3. Cover and cook on low-heat setting for 6 to 7 hours or on high-heat setting for 3 to 3½ hours.

4. Before serving, stir in vinegar. Season to taste with additional salt and pepper. Garnish with reserved fennel tops.

Per serving: 273 cal., 10 g total fat (3 g sat. fat), 19 mg chol., 776 mg sodium, 30 g carb., 13 g fiber, 17 g pro.

Ham with Carrots and Parsnips

Scoring the top of the ham dresses it up for serving and lets the flavor-packed cooking juices penetrate the meat.

Prep: 10 minutes
Cook: 8 to 9 hours (low) or 4 to 4½ hours (high)
Stand: 10 minutes
Makes 8 servings

1	16-ounce package peeled baby carrots
1	pound parsnips, peeled and cut into ½-inch-thick slices
1	2- to 2½-pound boneless cooked ham portion
1	cup apple juice or apple cider
¼	cup packed brown sugar
¼	cup honey mustard
⅛	teaspoon ground cloves

1. In a 5- to 6-quart slow cooker, combine carrots and parsnips.

2. If desired, score both sides of meat in a diamond pattern by making shallow diagonal cuts at 1-inch intervals. Place meat on top of vegetables in cooker. In a small bowl, combine apple juice, brown sugar, mustard, and cloves. Pour over mixture in cooker.

3. Cover and cook on low-heat setting for 8 to 9 hours or on high-heat setting for 4 to 4½ hours.

4. Remove meat from cooker; cover and let stand for 10 minutes. Meanwhile, using a slotted spoon, transfer vegetables to a large bowl. If desired, use a potato masher to mash vegetables, adding some of the liquid, if necessary, to moisten. Slice meat and serve with vegetables.

Per serving: 315 cal., 12 g total fat (4 g sat. fat), 65 mg chol., 1,581 mg sodium, 30 g carb., 4 g fiber, 21 g pro.

Smoked Sausage-Lentil Soup

Fresh fennel adds a tantalizing hint of **licorice** flavor to this full-bodied **sausage,** lentil, and carrot soup. For extra **pizzazz** use hot-style sausage.

Pork with Parsnips and Pears

Perfect for a meal on a blustery fall day, this pork dish gets its **exceptional** flavor from a **port wine sauce** that's loaded with garlic, rosemary, and thyme.

Pork with Parsnips and Pears

Bartlett and Bosc pears work well with this pork roast because they hold their shape during cooking.

Prep: 30 minutes
Cook: 11 to 12 hours (low) or 5½ to 6 hours (high)
Makes 8 to 10 servings

- 1   2½- to 3-pound boneless pork top loin roast (single loin)
- 1   tablespoon cooking oil
- 1½   pounds parsnips and/or carrots, peeled and cut into 1½- to 2-inch pieces*
- 2   medium pears, peeled, quartered, and cored (stems intact, if desired) (about 2 cups)
- 2   tablespoons quick-cooking tapioca
- 1   tablespoon bottled minced garlic or 6 cloves garlic, minced
- 1   teaspoon dried rosemary, crushed
- 1   teaspoon dried thyme, crushed
- ½   teaspoon salt
- ¼   teaspoon ground black pepper
- ½   cup port wine or apple juice
     Salt
     Ground black pepper

1. In a large skillet, brown meat on all sides in hot oil. Place parsnips and/or carrots and pears in a 5- to 6-quart slow cooker; sprinkle with tapioca. Place meat on top of parsnips and pears; sprinkle meat with garlic, rosemary, thyme, the ½ teaspoon salt, and the ¼ teaspoon pepper. Pour wine over all.

2. Cover and cook on low-heat setting for 11 to 12 hours or on high-heat setting for 5½ to 6 hours.

3. Transfer meat to serving platter, reserving cooking liquid; use a slotted spoon to transfer parsnips and/or carrots and pears to serving platter.

4. Slice meat. Season sauce to taste with salt and pepper. Serve with meat, vegetables, and pears.

Per serving: 340 cal., 9 g total fat (3 g sat. fat), 78 mg chol., 292 mg sodium, 27 g carb., 6 g fiber, 32 g pro.

*Note: Cut any thick carrot or parsnip pieces in half lengthwise.

Apricot Pulled Pork

Prep: 20 minutes
Cook: 8 to 10 hours (low) or 4 to 5 hours (high)
Makes 8 servings

-   Nonstick cooking spray
- 1   3- to 3½-pound boneless pork shoulder roast
- 1   10-ounce jar apricot spreadable fruit
- 1   cup bottled hot-style barbecue sauce
- ½   cup chopped sweet onion (such as Vidalia, Maui, or Walla Walla)
- ½   cup snipped dried apricots
- 8   kaiser rolls or hamburger buns

1. Lightly coat a 3½- or 4-quart slow cooker with cooking spray. Trim fat from meat. If necessary, cut meat to fit into cooker. Place meat in prepared cooker. In a medium bowl, combine spreadable fruit, barbecue sauce, onion, and dried apricots. Pour over meat in cooker.

2. Cover and cook on low heat-setting for 8 to 10 hours or on high-heat setting for 4 to 5 hours.

3. Transfer meat to a cutting board. Using two forks, gently shred the meat. In a large bowl, combine shredded meat and some of the sauce from the cooker. Serve meat mixture on kaiser rolls. Pass remaining sauce.

Per serving: 553 cal., 17 g total fat (5 g sat. fat), 116 mg chol., 685 mg sodium, 61 g carb., 2 g fiber, 40 g pro.

Potatoes, Sauerkraut, and Sausage Supper

Some good crusty bread and a selection of your favorite mustards are perfect serve-alongs for this robust, German-style meal.

Prep: 20 minutes
Cook: 5 to 6 hours (low) or 2½ to 3 hours (high), plus 30 minutes on high
Makes 8 servings

1	20-ounce package refrigerated diced potatoes with onions
1	cup chopped green sweet pepper
1	cup chopped carrot
1½	pounds cooked smoked Polish sausage, cut into 2-inch pieces
⅔	cup apple juice or apple cider
1	tablespoon cider vinegar
½	teaspoon caraway seeds
¼	teaspoon salt
¼	teaspoon ground black pepper
1	14- to 16-ounce can sauerkraut, drained

1. In a 4½- to 5½-quart slow cooker, combine potatoes, sweet pepper, and carrot. Add sausage.

2. In a small bowl, stir together apple juice, cider vinegar, caraway seeds, salt, and black pepper. Pour over mixture in cooker.

3. Cover and cook on low-heat setting for 5 to 6 hours or on high-heat setting for 2½ to 3 hours.

4. If using low-heat setting, turn to high-heat setting. Stir in sauerkraut. Cover and cook for 30 minutes more. To serve, transfer mixture to a serving bowl.

Per serving: 374 cal., 25 g total fat (9 g sat. fat), 60 mg chol., 1,291 mg sodium, 24 g carb., 4 g fiber, 14 g pro.

Ham and Scalloped Potatoes

This old-fashioned favorite has been updated for today's busy cooks with frozen hash browns, canned soup, and ham and pimiento purchased already diced. It goes together in minutes but simmers slow and easy all day.

Prep: 10 minutes
Cook: 7 to 9 hours (low) or 3½ to 4 hours (high)
Makes 6 servings

1	28-ounce package loose-pack frozen hash brown potatoes with onion and peppers
2	cups diced cooked ham (10 ounces)
1	2-ounce jar diced pimiento, drained
¼	teaspoon ground black pepper
1	11-ounce can condensed cheddar cheese soup
¾	cup milk
1	tablespoon snipped fresh parsley

1. In a 3½-quart slow cooker, combine frozen hash brown potatoes, ham, pimiento, and pepper.

2. In a medium bowl, combine cheddar cheese soup and milk; pour over the potato mixture in cooker. Stir to combine.

3. Cover and cook on low-heat setting for 7 to 9 hours or on high-heat setting for 3½ to 4 hours. Stir in parsley.

Per serving: 241 cal., 9 g total fat (3 g sat. fat), 37 mg chol., 1,180 mg sodium, 30 g carb., 3 g fiber, 16 g pro.

Potatoes, Sauerkraut, and Sausage Supper

Meatball Cassoulet

Cassoulet is a rustic stew from France that's made with **white beans** and a variety of meats. Work-saving frozen **meatballs** make this version extra **easy.**

Sweet-Sour Pork Stew

Sweet-and-sour pork can be a lot of work to prepare because the pork is battered and fried. With this easy-fixing stew, you can enjoy all the same flavors but skip the kitchen time.

Prep: 25 minutes
Cook: 7 to 9 hours (low) or 3½ to 4½ hours (high)
Makes 4 to 6 servings

1½	pounds lean pork stew meat
3	tablespoons all-purpose flour
½	teaspoon salt
¼	teaspoon ground black pepper
1	tablespoon cooking oil
1	cup chopped onion
5	medium carrots, cut into ½-inch-thick slices
1	14½-ounce can diced tomatoes, undrained
¼	cup packed brown sugar
¼	cup vinegar
2	tablespoons quick-cooking tapioca
1	tablespoon Worcestershire sauce

1. Cut meat into 1-inch pieces. In a resealable plastic bag, combine flour, salt, and pepper. Add meat pieces, a few at a time, shaking to coat. In a large skillet, cook half of the meat in hot oil until brown. Transfer meat to a 3½- or 4-quart slow cooker. Add remaining meat and the onion to skillet. Cook until meat is brown and onion is tender. Drain off fat. Transfer meat mixture to cooker. Add carrots.

2. In a medium bowl, combine undrained tomatoes, brown sugar, vinegar, tapioca, and Worcestershire sauce. Pour over mixture in cooker.

3. Cover and cook on low-heat setting for 7 to 9 hours or on high-heat setting for 3½ to 4½ hours.
Per serving: 394 cal., 10 g total fat (3 g sat. fat), 95 mg chol., 619 mg sodium, 41 g carb., 4 g fiber, 34 g pro.

Meatball Cassoulet

Navy or cannellini (white kidney) beans are tasty alternatives to the Great Northerns.

Prep: 25 minutes
Cook: 8 to 9 hours (low) or 4 to 4½ hours (high)
Makes 4 or 5 servings

2	15-ounce cans Great Northern beans, rinsed and drained
2	cups tomato juice
1	12-ounce package frozen cooked Italian meatballs, thawed
8	ounces cooked smoked turkey sausage or Polish sausage, halved lengthwise and sliced
1	cup finely chopped carrot
1	cup chopped celery
1	cup chopped onion
1	tablespoon Worcestershire sauce
½	teaspoon dried basil, crushed
½	teaspoon dried oregano, crushed
½	teaspoon paprika

1. In a 3½- or 4-quart slow cooker, combine beans, tomato juice, meatballs, sausage, carrot, celery, onion, Worcestershire sauce, basil, oregano, and paprika.

2. Cover and cook on low-heat setting for 8 to 9 hours or on high-heat setting for 4 to 4½ hours.
Per serving: 657 cal., 25 g total fat (11 g sat. fat), 93 mg chol., 1,655 mg sodium, 68 g carb., 17 g fiber, 42 g pro.

Pork and Lentil Cassoulet

Lentils replace the traditional white beans in this colorful pork version of **cassoulet** that's seasoned with garlic and rosemary as well as a **medley of vegetables.**

Pork Chops with Orange-Dijon Sauce

Orange marmalade laced with Dijon mustard provides a sweet yet snappy glaze for these boneless chops.

Prep: 15 minutes
Cook: 6 to 7 hours (low) or 3 to 3½ hours (high)
Makes 6 servings

6	boneless pork sirloin chops, cut 1 inch thick
	Salt
	Ground black pepper
½	teaspoon dried thyme, crushed
1	cup orange marmalade
⅓	cup Dijon-style mustard
¼	cup water

1. Sprinkle chops lightly with salt and pepper. Sprinkle chops with thyme. Place chops in a 3½- or 4-quart slow cooker. In a small bowl, combine orange marmalade and mustard. Remove 2 tablespoons of the marmalade mixture; cover and refrigerate. Stir the water into remaining marmalade mixture. Pour over chops in cooker.

2. Cover and cook on low-heat setting for 6 to 7 hours or on high-heat setting for 3 to 3½ hours.

3. Transfer chops to a serving platter, discarding the cooking liquid. Spread reserved marmalade mixture over chops.

Per serving: 409 cal., 15 g total fat (5 g sat. fat), 166 mg chol., 212 mg sodium, 9 g carb., 1 g fiber, 56 g pro.

Pork and Lentil Cassoulet

The disk-shaped brown lentils lend a nutty note to this French-style stew.

Prep: 25 minutes
Cook: 10 to 12 hours (low) or 4½ to 5½ hours (high)
Makes 4 servings

12	ounces boneless pork shoulder
1	large onion, cut into wedges
2	cloves garlic, minced
2	teaspoons cooking oil
2½	cups water
1	14½-ounce can tomatoes, undrained, cut up
4	medium carrots and/or parsnips, peeled and cut into ½-inch-thick slices
2	stalks celery, thinly sliced
¾	cup dry brown lentils, rinsed and drained
1½	teaspoons dried rosemary, crushed
1	teaspoon instant beef bouillon granules
¼	teaspoon salt
¼	teaspoon ground black pepper
	Fresh rosemary sprigs (optional)

1. Trim fat from meat. Cut meat into ¾-inch cubes. In a large nonstick skillet, cook meat, onion, and garlic in hot oil until meat is brown and onion is tender. Transfer mixture to a 3½- or 4-quart slow cooker. Add the water, undrained tomatoes, carrots and/or parsnips, celery, lentils, rosemary, bouillon granules, salt, and pepper.

2. Cover and cook on low-heat setting for 10 to 12 hours or on high-heat setting for 4½ to 5½ hours.

3. If desired, garnish with fresh rosemary sprigs.

Per serving: 354 cal., 12 g total fat (3 g sat. fat), 37 mg chol., 641 mg sodium, 37 g carb., 5 g fiber, 26 g pro.

Curried Split Pea Soup

If your supermarket doesn't routinely carry smoked pork hocks, ask the butcher to order some for you.

Prep: 25 minutes
Cook: 9 to 11 hours (low) or 4½ to 5½ hours (high)
Makes 6 servings

Curried Split Pea Soup

1	pound dry split peas, rinsed and drained
1	pound smoked pork hocks or meaty ham bone
1½	cups cubed cooked ham (about 8 ounces)
1½	cups coarsely chopped celery
1	cup chopped onion
1	cup coarsely chopped carrot
3	to 4 teaspoons curry powder
1	tablespoon dried marjoram, crushed
2	bay leaves
¼	teaspoon ground black pepper
6	cups water

1. In a 5- to 6-quart slow cooker, combine split peas, pork hocks, ham, celery, onion, carrot, curry powder, marjoram, bay leaves, and pepper. Stir in the water.

2. Cover and cook on low-heat setting for 9 to 11 hours or on high-heat setting for 4½ to 5½ hours.

3. Discard bay leaves. Remove pork hocks. When pork hocks are cool enough to handle, remove meat from bones; discard bones. Coarsely chop meat. Return meat to soup.

Per serving: 379 cal., 6 g total fat (2 g sat. fat), 32 mg chol., 788 mg sodium, 54 g carb., 22 g fiber, 29 g pro.

Sweet and Spicy Lamb Wraps

Prep: 30 minutes
Cook: 10 to 12 hours (low) or 5 to 6 hours (high)
Makes 8 sandwiches

- 1 2½- to 3-pound boneless lamb shoulder roast
- 1 large onion, cut into wedges
- ½ cup mango chutney
- ½ cup chicken broth
- 1 tablespoon cider vinegar
- 1 teaspoon crushed red pepper
- ¼ cup mayonnaise or salad dressing
- ¼ cup plain yogurt
- 2 tablespoons mango chutney, large pieces snipped
- ½ teaspoon curry powder
- 8 pita bread rounds
- 3 cups shredded lettuce
- 1 medium tomato, seeded and chopped

1. Trim fat from meat. If necessary, cut meat to fit into a 3½- or 4-quart slow cooker. Place onion in the cooker; add meat.

2. In a small bowl, stir together the ½ cup chutney, the broth, vinegar, and crushed red pepper. Pour over mixture in cooker.

3. Cover and cook on low-heat setting for 10 to 12 hours or on high-heat setting for 5 to 6 hours.

4. Remove meat and onion from cooker, reserving cooking liquid. Using two forks, shred the meat. If desired, stir in enough cooking liquid to moisten. For sauce, in a bowl, stir together mayonnaise, yogurt, the 2 tablespoons chutney, and the curry powder.

5. To serve, place meat mixture along centers of pita rounds. Top with lettuce and tomato; drizzle with sauce. Fold both sides of each pita up around filling.
Per Serving: 619 cal., 30 g total fat (11 g sat. fat), 100 mg chol., 541 mg sodium, 54 g carb., 3 g fiber, 31 g pro.

Greek Lamb with Spinach and Orzo

Bold Mediterranean flavors come alive in this robust dish that showcases chunks of lamb tossed with spinach, orzo, and feta cheese.
Prep: 25 minutes
Cook: 8 to 10 hours (low) or 4 to 5 hours (high)
Makes 8 servings

- 1 3- to 3½-pound lamb shoulder roast (bone-in)
- 1 tablespoon dried oregano, crushed
- 1 tablespoon finely shredded lemon peel
- 4 cloves garlic, minced
- ¼ teaspoon salt
- ¼ cup lemon juice
- 1 10-ounce bag prewashed fresh spinach, chopped
- 5 cups cooked orzo
- 4 ounces feta cheese, crumbled

1. Trim fat from meat. If necessary, cut meat to fit into a 3½- to 6-quart slow cooker. In a small bowl, combine oregano, lemon peel, garlic, and salt. Sprinkle oregano mixture evenly over meat; rub in with your fingers. Place meat in cooker. Sprinkle meat with lemon juice.

2. Cover and cook on low-heat setting for 8 to 10 hours or on high-heat setting for 4 to 5 hours.

3. Remove meat from cooker, reserving cooking juices in cooker. Remove meat from bones; discard bones and fat. Chop meat; set aside. Add spinach to cooking juices in cooker, stirring until spinach is wilted. Add chopped meat, cooked orzo, and feta to spinach mixture; stir to mix.
Per serving: 409 cal., 16 g total fat (7 g sat. fat), 120 mg chol., 338 mg sodium, 25 g carb., 5 g fiber, 38 g pro.

Country Bean Stew

A trio of meats—lamb, Italian sausage, and ham—make this tomatoey **bean stew** filling and **satisfying.**

Country Bean Stew

If you enjoy bold, full-flavor dishes, use hot Italian sausage in place of the regular.

Prep: 30 minutes
Stand: 1 hour
Cook: 7 to 8 hours (low), plus 15 minutes, or 3½ to 4 hours (high), plus 15 minutes
Makes 6 servings

6	**cups water**
2	**cups dry Great Northern beans**
3	**large carrots, coarsely chopped**
12	**ounces lean boneless lamb, cut into cubes**
8	**ounces bulk Italian sausage**
3	**medium onions, coarsely chopped**
3	**cloves garlic, minced**
3	**cups water**
1	**teaspoon instant beef bouillon granules**
½	**teaspoon dried thyme, crushed**
½	**teaspoon dried oregano, crushed**
¼	**cup dry red wine**
⅓	**cup tomato paste (½ of a 6-ounce can)**
½	**cup cubed cooked ham**
¼	**cup snipped fresh parsley**

1. In a large saucepan, combine the 6 cups water and the dry beans. Bring to boiling; reduce heat. Simmer for 10 minutes. Remove from heat. Cover and let stand for 1 hour. Drain beans; rinse with cold water and drain again.

2. In a 4- to 5-quart slow cooker, combine beans and carrots. In a large skillet, cook lamb, sausage, onions, and garlic over medium heat until sausage is brown, breaking up sausage as it cooks. Drain off fat. Transfer meat mixture to cooker. Stir in the 3 cups water, the bouillon granules, thyme, and oregano.

3. Cover and cook on low-heat setting for 7 to 8 hours or on high-heat setting for 3½ to 4 hours.

4. In a small bowl, stir wine into tomato paste; add to mixture in cooker along with ham and parsley. Cover and cook for 15 minutes more.

Per serving: 470 cal., 12 g total fat (5 g sat. fat), 69 mg chol., 732 mg sodium, 51 g carb., 15 g fiber, 35 g pro.

Lamb Shanks with Polenta

Lamb foreshanks are smaller than hindshanks, making them perfect for the slow cooker.

Prep: 15 minutes
Cook: 11 to 12 hours (low) or 5½ to 6 hours (high)
Makes 4 to 6 servings

1	**pound boiling onions, peeled**
½	**cup pitted Greek black olives**
4	**meaty lamb foreshanks (about 4 pounds total) or meaty veal shank crosscuts (about 3 pounds total)**
4	**cloves garlic, minced**
2	**teaspoons dried rosemary, crushed**
½	**teaspoon salt**
¼	**teaspoon ground black pepper**
1	**cup chicken broth**
1¼	**cups quick-cooking polenta**

1. Place onions and olives in a 5- to 6-quart slow cooker. Arrange meat in cooker. Sprinkle with garlic, rosemary, salt, and pepper. Pour broth over all.

2. Cover and cook on low-heat setting for 11 to 12 hours or on high-heat setting for 5½ to 6 hours.

3. To serve, prepare polenta according to package directions. Using a slotted spoon, transfer meat, onions, and olives to a serving dish and pass with polenta. If you wish to serve cooking liquid with meat, skim fat and discard; strain liquid.

Per serving: 701 cal., 21 g total fat (7 g sat. fat), 136 mg chol., 768 mg sodium, 79 g carb., 12 g fiber, 46 g pro.

Moroccan Lamb

Be sure to serve plenty of pita bread to go along with this zesty lamb dish.

Prep: 25 minutes
Cook: 8 to 9 hours (low) or 4 to 4½ hours (high)
Makes 6 servings

2	pounds boneless lamb shoulder roast
2	tablespoons olive oil
1	medium onion, chopped
2	cloves garlic, minced
1	tablespoon grated fresh ginger
1	6-ounce package long grain and wild rice mix
1	cup dried apricots
½	cup raisins
½	cup dried tart cherries
2	medium yellow summer squash, cut into 1-inch pieces (2½ cups)
1	8-ounce package fresh mushrooms, halved or quartered
½	teaspoon coarsely ground black pepper
¼	teaspoon ground cinnamon
⅛	to ¼ teaspoon cayenne pepper
1½	cups water

1. Trim fat from lamb. Cut meat into 1-inch pieces. In a large skillet, brown meat, half at a time, in hot oil over medium heat. Transfer meat to a 4½- or 5-quart slow cooker.* Layer in order: onion, garlic, ginger, rice mix and contents of seasoning packet, dried apricots, raisins, dried cherries, squash, and mushrooms. Sprinkle with black pepper, cinnamon, and cayenne pepper; pour the water over all.

2. Cover and cook on low-heat setting for 8 to 9 hours or on low-heat setting for 4 to 4½ hours.

3. Stir gently before serving.

Per serving: 472 cal., 12 g total fat (3 g sat. fat), 95 mg chol., 505 mg sodium, 58 g carb., 5 g fiber, 37 g pro.

*Note: To make cleanup easier, arrange a slow-cooker liner in the cooker before adding meat.

Add a Finishing Touch

A sensational soup or stew gets even better if you add a little something extra for garnish. Try one of these options to help boost the flavor, texture, color, and eye appeal of any meal in a bowl.

• Croutons, popcorn, coarsely crushed tortilla chips, crispy fried wonton strips, bite-size fish-shape crackers, toast points, and squares of puff pastry all lend crunch.
• Add a hint of herb flavor with some snipped fresh herb, sliced green onions, or snipped chives.
• Perk up the color of creamy soups and stews with chopped hard-cooked egg, tomato, sweet pepper, avocado, or cooked beets. Or sprinkle on crumbled cooked bacon or sliced olives.
• Cool down spicy mixtures with some sour cream, plain yogurt, or crème fraîche.

• Spoon on a dab of bottled pesto, roasted garlic, or tapenade.
• Grate on lemon, lime, or orange peel for a fresh note. Or float citrus slices or citrus peel curls.
• Toast pine nuts, sliced almonds, pecan pieces, chopped pistachios, or chopped hazelnuts for a tasty topping.
• Shred, shave, or grate Parmesan or Romano cheese on top of Italian-seasoned soups. Or add a little chopped dried tomato.
• Use sliced pickled or fresh chile peppers or bottled salsa to add pizzazz to Mexican-style dishes.
• Sprinkle on shredded cheddar or Monterey Jack cheese or a few crumbles of goat or blue cheese.
• Float some edible flowers on top of a creamy soup for an elegant touch.

Moroccan Lamb

An intriguing blend of rice, apricots, **raisins,** cherries, summer squash, and mushrooms—all flavored with **cinnamon** and **cayenne**—accompanies this savory lamb.

quick side salads

Add a refreshing note to slow-cooked meals with these simple, but tempting, salads. Because they're made with easy-to-find, easy-to-use ingredients, they go together in minutes.

Asian Pea Pod Salad
Makes 6 servings

In a large salad bowl, toss together 6 cups torn romaine and 2 cups fresh pea pods, trimmed and halved crosswise. In a small bowl, stir together 1/3 cup bottled Italian salad dressing and 1 tablespoon bottled hoisin sauce. Pour over romaine mixture; toss to coat. Sprinkle with 1 tablespoon sesame seeds.

Per serving: 98 cal., 7 g total fat (1 g sat. fat), 0 mg chol., 153 mg sodium, 6 g carb., 2 g fiber, 2 g pro.

Ginger-Sesame Slaw
Makes 6 servings

In a large bowl, stir together 4 cups thinly bias-sliced bok choy, 2 cups carrot ribbons or sliced carrots, 1 cup sliced radishes, and 2 teaspoons grated fresh ginger. Stir in enough bottled Oriental sesame salad dressing (1/4 to 1/2 cup) to moisten. Serve immediately or cover and chill for up to 1 hour.

Per serving: 69 cal., 4 g total fat (1 g sat. fat), 0 mg chol., 121 mg sodium, 8 g carb., 2 g fiber, 2 g pro.

Tomato and Cheese Toss
Makes 6 servings

In a medium bowl, combine 1 pound coarsely chopped roma tomatoes; 4 ounces mozzarella or provolone cheese, cubed; and 2/3 cup pimiento-stuffed green olives. Pour 1/4 cup bottled Italian vinaigrette salad dressing or Italian salad dressing over tomato mixture; toss to coat. Let stand for 5 minutes before serving.

Per serving: 126 cal., 10 g total fat (3 g sat. fat), 11 mg chol., 510 mg sodium, 5 g carb., 1 g fiber, 5 g pro.

Orange Dream Fruit Salad
Makes 4 to 6 servings

In a medium bowl, combine 1 cup chopped, peeled, seeded mango or papaya; one 11-ounce can mandarin orange sections, drained; and 1 cup seedless red and/or green grapes, halved. In a small bowl, stir together 1/2 cup orange-flavored yogurt and 1/4 teaspoon poppy seeds. Gently stir yogurt mixture into the fruit mixture until combined.

Per serving: 136 cal., 1 g total fat (0 g sat. fat), 2 mg chol., 26 mg sodium, 32 g carb., 2 g fiber, 2 g pro.

Mango-Broccoli Salad
Makes 8 servings

In a large bowl, combine 4 cups fresh broccoli florets; 1 large mango, peeled, pitted, and sliced; 1/2 cup cashews; and 1/2 cup thinly sliced red onion. In a small bowl, combine 3/4 cup bottled buttermilk ranch salad dressing, 3 tablespoons orange juice, and 1 tablespoon prepared horseradish. Add to broccoli mixture; toss to mix. Drain one 11-ounce can mandarin orange sections; arrange orange sections on top of salad.

Per serving: 214 cal., 16 g total fat (3 g sat. fat), 4 mg chol., 205 mg sodium, 17 g carb., 2 g fiber, 3 g pro.

Tomato and Mint Salad
Makes 6 servings

For dressing, sprinkle a cutting board with a pinch of salt. Using the flat blade of a knife, crush 1 large clove garlic into the salt. Finely chop the garlic into the salt to create a chunky paste. In a screw-top jar, combine the garlic paste, 1/4 cup olive oil, 1/2 teaspoon finely shredded lemon peel, 1 tablespoon lemon juice, and 1 tablespoon white wine vinegar or cider vinegar. Cover; shake well.

Slice 3 large red and/or yellow tomatoes crosswise; place half of the tomato slices in a single layer on a serving platter. Top with 1/4 cup snipped fresh mint. Drizzle half of the dressing over all. Top

with remaining tomato slices and another 1/4 cup snipped fresh mint. Sprinkle with freshly ground black pepper; drizzle with remaining dressing. If desired, garnish with fresh mint leaves.

Per serving: 102 cal., 9 g total fat (1 g sat. fat), 0 mg chol., 29 mg sodium, 5 g carb., 1 g fiber, 1 g pro.

Marinated Bean Salad
Makes 8 servings

Cook one 9-ounce package frozen cut green beans according to package directions; drain. Rinse with cold water and drain again.

In a large bowl, stir together the cooked green beans; two 15- to 19-ounce cans navy, red kidney, and/or white kidney (cannellini) beans, rinsed and drained; and 1/2 cup thinly sliced red onion.

In a small bowl, stir together 1/2 cup bottled balsamic vinaigrette salad dressing and 3 tablespoons molasses. Pour over bean mixture; toss to coat.

Cover and chill salad for 4 to 24 hours. Serve salad with a slotted spoon.

Per serving: 200 cal., 5 g total fat (1 g sat. fat), 0 mg chol., 655 mg sodium, 32 g carb., 6 g fiber, 9 g pro.

Spinach-Cucumber Salad
Makes 4 servings

In a large salad bowl, combine one 6-ounce package fresh baby spinach or one 8-ounce package torn mixed salad greens, 1/2 cup thinly sliced English cucumber, and 1/4 cup coarsely shredded red radish or daikon. Pour 1/2 cup bottled tahini salad dressing or oil-and-vinegar salad dressing over salad; toss to coat. Sprinkle with 1 tablespoon toasted sesame seeds.

Per serving: 167 cal., 14 g total fat (1 g sat. fat), 0 mg chol., 392 mg sodium, 6 g carb., 4 g fiber, 3 g pro.

Fresh Fruit with Citrus Dressing
Makes 6 servings

Cut up enough assorted fresh fruit, such as pineapple, strawberries, kiwifruit, and/or papaya, to measure 4 cups. For dressing, in a medium bowl, whisk together 1/4 cup orange juice, 1 tablespoon snipped fresh mint, and 1 teaspoon honey. Add cut-up fruit to dressing; toss lightly to coat.

Per serving: 58 cal., 0 g total fat (0 g sat. fat), 0 mg chol., 3 mg sodium, 13 g carb., 2 g fiber, 1 g pro.

Cacciatore-Style Chicken

poultry
and fish

Coming home to the tantalizing aroma of a chicken, turkey, or fish dinner waiting in the slow cooker is a luxury you can enjoy often with these delectable fix-and-forget recipes.

Cacciatore-Style Chicken

Similar to the familiar Italian classic, this meal-in-a-pot is brims with onions, mushrooms, and seasoned tomatoes.

Prep: 25 minutes   **Cook:** 6 to 7 hours (low) or 3 to 3½ hours (high), plus 15 minutes on high

Makes 6 servings

2	cups sliced fresh mushrooms
1	cup sliced celery
1	cup chopped carrot
2	medium onions, cut into wedges
1	yellow, green, or red sweet pepper, cut into strips
4	cloves garlic, minced
12	chicken drumsticks, skinned (about 3½ pounds total)
½	cup chicken broth
¼	cup dry white wine
2	tablespoons quick-cooking tapioca
2	bay leaves
1	teaspoon dried oregano, crushed
1	teaspoon sugar
½	teaspoon salt
¼	teaspoon ground black pepper
1	14½-ounce can diced tomatoes, undrained
⅓	cup tomato paste
	Hot cooked pasta or rice
	Shredded basil (optional)

1. In a 5- to 6-quart slow cooker, combine mushrooms, celery, carrot, onions, sweet pepper, and garlic. Place chicken drumsticks on vegetables. Add broth, wine, tapioca, bay leaves, oregano, sugar, salt, and pepper.

2. Cover and cook on low-heat setting for 6 to 7 hours or on high-heat setting for 3 to 3½ hours.

3. Remove chicken and keep warm. Discard bay leaves. If using low-heat setting, turn to high-heat setting. Stir in undrained tomatoes and tomato paste. Cover and cook for 15 minutes more. To serve, spoon vegetable mixture over chicken and pasta. If desired, garnish with basil.

Per serving: 345 cal., 7 g total fat (2 g sat. fat), 81 mg chol., 606 mg sodium, 37 g carb., 4 g fiber, 32 g pro.

Chicken Jambalaya

The spicy Cajun flavor of this slow-cooked Louisiana favorite will put a zip in your day.

Prep: 15 minutes
Cook: 5 to 6 hours (low) or 2½ to 3 hours (high), plus 45 minutes on high
Makes 6 servings

- 8 ounces skinless, boneless chicken breast halves
- 1 16-ounce package frozen (yellow, green, and red) peppers and onion stir-fry vegetables
- 8 ounces smoked turkey sausage, halved lengthwise and cut into ½-inch-thick slices
- 2 cups water
- 1 14½-ounce can diced tomatoes with jalapeño chile peppers, undrained
- 1 8-ounce package jambalaya rice mix

1. Cut chicken into ½-inch strips. Place frozen vegetables in a 3½- or 4-quart slow cooker. Top with chicken strips and turkey sausage slices. Add the water, undrained tomatoes, and, if present, seasoning packet from rice. Set dry rice mix aside.

2. Cover and cook on low-heat setting for 5 to 6 hours or on high-heat setting for 2½ to 3 hours.

3. Stir in dry rice mix. If using low-heat setting, turn to high-heat setting. Cover and cook about 45 minutes more or until most of the liquid is absorbed and rice is tender.

Per serving: 265 cal., 4 g total fat (1 g sat. fat), 47 mg chol., 1,118 mg sodium, 37 g carb., 2 g fiber, 19 g pro.

Easy Chicken Rarebit

The cheese pasta sauce and the Worcestershire sauce make this dish reminiscent of Welsh rarebit.

Prep: 20 minutes
Cook: 4 to 5 hours (low) or 2 to 2½ hours (high)
Makes 6 servings

- 1¾ pounds skinless, boneless chicken breast halves
- 1 14- to 16-ounce jar cheddar cheese pasta sauce
- 1 tablespoon Worcestershire sauce
- 1 large onion, halved crosswise and thinly sliced
- 6 pumpernickel or rye buns, split and toasted, or 6 slices pumpernickel or rye bread, toasted and halved diagonally
- 4 slices bacon, crisp-cooked, drained, and crumbled (optional)
- 1 tomato, chopped (optional)
  Kosher dill pickles (optional)

1. Cut chicken diagonally into ½-inch-thick slices; set aside. In a 3½- or 4-quart slow cooker, stir together pasta sauce and Worcestershire sauce. Add onion and chicken slices.

2. Cover and cook on low-heat setting for 4 to 5 hours or on high-heat setting for 2 to 2½ hours.

3. To serve, spoon chicken and sauce mixture over bun halves. If desired, sprinkle with crumbled bacon and tomato. Serve with dill pickles, if desired.

Per serving: 340 cal., 12 g total fat (4 g sat. fat), 102 mg chol., 823 mg sodium, 21 g carb., 3 g fiber, 36 g pro.

Easy Chicken Rarebit

Chicken and Dumplings

Prep: 25 minutes
Cook: 8 to 10 hours (low) or 4 to 5 hours (high), plus 25 minutes on high
Makes 8 servings

Chicken and Dumplings

2	cups chopped carrots
2	cups chopped potatoes
1½	cups chopped parsnips
1	clove garlic, minced
2	bay leaves
1	teaspoon dried sage, crushed
¾	teaspoon salt
¼	teaspoon ground black pepper
2	pounds boneless, skinless chicken thighs, cut into 1-inch pieces
1	14-ounce can chicken broth
1	10¾-ounce can condensed cream of chicken soup
2	tablespoons water
1	tablespoon cornstarch
½	cup all-purpose flour
½	cup shredded cheddar cheese (2 ounces)
⅓	cup cornmeal
1	teaspoon baking powder
1	egg, beaten
2	tablespoons milk
2	tablespoons butter, melted

1. For stew, in a 4- or 5-quart slow cooker combine the carrots, potatoes, parsnips, garlic, bay leaves, sage, ½ teaspoon salt, and pepper. Place the chicken on top of the vegetables. In a medium bowl gradually whisk broth into soup. Pour over chicken.

2. Cover; cook on low-heat setting for 8 to 10 hours or on high-heat setting for 4 to 5 hours.

3. If using low-heat setting, turn slow cooker to high-heat setting. With a wooden spoon, stir stew. Remove bay leaves; discard. In a small bowl combine water and cornstarch; stir into stew until combined.

4. For dumplings, in a medium mixing bowl combine flour, cheese, cornmeal, baking powder, and the remaining ¼ teaspoon salt. In a small bowl combine egg, milk, and melted butter. Add egg mixture to flour mixture. Stir with a fork until moistened. Use 2 spoons to drop dough directly on top of stew.

5. Cover; cook for 25 to 30 minutes more or until a toothpick inserted into a dumpling comes out clean. (Do not lift cover during cooking.)

Per serving: 361 cal., 14 g total fat (6 g sat. fat), 140 mg chol., 948 mg sodium, 29 g carb., 4 g fiber, 29 g pro.

Greek Chicken with Couscous

Prep: 15 minutes
Cook: 5 to 6 hours (low) or 2½ to 3 hours (high)
Stand: 5 minutes
Makes 8 servings

2	**pounds skinless, boneless chicken breast halves**
2	**14½-ounce cans diced tomatoes with basil, oregano, and garlic, undrained**
1½	**cups water**
2	**6-ounce packages couscous with toasted pine nut mix**
1	**cup crumbled feta cheese (4 ounces)**
½	**cup pitted kalamata olives, coarsely chopped**

1. Cut chicken into ½-inch pieces. Place chicken in a 3½- or 4-quart slow cooker. Add undrained tomatoes and 1½ cups water.

2. Cover and cook on low-heat setting for 5 to 6 hours or on high-heat setting for 2½ to 3 hours. Stir in couscous. Cover and let stand for 5 minutes. Fluff couscous mixture with a fork.

3. To serve, on each of 8 dinner plates spoon couscous mixture. Sprinkle with feta cheese and olives.

Per serving: 377 cal., 8 g total fat (4 g sat. fat), 82 mg chol., 1,226 mg sodium, 41 g carb., 3 g fiber, 36 g pro.

Chicken and Noodles with Vegetables

Prep: 25 minutes
Cook: 8 to 9 hours (low) or 4 to 4½ hours (high)
Makes 6 servings

2	**cups sliced carrot (4 medium)**
1½	**cups chopped onion (3 medium)**
1	**cup sliced celery (2 stalks)**
2	**tablespoons snipped fresh parsley**
1	**bay leaf**
3	**medium chicken legs (drumstick-thigh portion) (about 2 pounds total), skinned**
2	**10.75-ounce cans reduced-fat and reduced-sodium condensed cream of chicken soup**
½	**cup water**
1	**teaspoon dried thyme, crushed**
¼	**teaspoon ground black pepper**
5	**cups dried wide noodles (10 ounces)**
1	**cup frozen peas**
	Salt (optional)

1. In a 3½- or 4-quart slow cooker, stir together carrot, onion, celery, parsley, and bay leaf. Place chicken on top of vegetables. In a large bowl, stir together soup, the water, thyme, and the ¼ teaspoon pepper. Pour over chicken in cooker.

2. Cover and cook on low-heat setting for 8 to 9 hours or on high-heat setting for 4 to 4½ hours. Remove chicken from slow cooker; cool slightly. Discard bay leaf.

3. Cook noodles according to package directions; drain. Meanwhile, stir frozen peas into mixture in slow cooker. Remove chicken from bones; discard bones. Shred or chop meat; stir into mixture in slow cooker.

4. To serve, spoon chicken mixture over noodles. If desired, season to taste with salt and additional pepper.

Per serving: 406 cal., 7 g total fat (2 g sat. fat), 122 mg chol., 532 mg sodium, 56 g carbo., 5 g dietary fiber, 28 g protein.

Chicken with Creamy Chive Sauce

Italian salad dressing mix, golden mushroom soup, wine, and flavored cream cheese create this **flavorful** chicken dish. If you like, serve over pasta or rice with a **generous portion** of sauce.

Chicken with Creamy Chive Sauce

Prep: 15 minutes
Cook: 4 to 5 hours (low)
Makes 6 servings

  6 skinless, boneless chicken breast halves (about 1½ pounds total)
  ¼ cup butter
  1 0.7-ounce package Italian salad dressing mix
  1 10¾-ounce can condensed golden mushroom soup
  ½ cup dry white wine
  ½ of an 8-ounce tub cream cheese with chives and onion
     Snipped fresh chives (optional)

1. Place chicken in a 3½- or 4-quart slow cooker. In a medium saucepan, melt the butter. Stir in the dry Italian salad dressing mix. Add mushroom soup, wine, and cream cheese, stirring until combined. Pour over the chicken.

2. Cover; cook on low-heat setting for 4 to 5 hours. Serve chicken with sauce. If desired, sprinkle with fresh chives.

Per serving: 310 cal., 17 g total fat (9 g sat. fat), 110 mg chol., 1,043 mg sodium, 6 g carb., 0 g fiber, 28 g pro.

Green Chile Taco Salad

Any leftover mixture can be used to make nachos another day.
Prep: 15 minutes
Cook: 6 to 8 hours (low) or 3 to 3½ hours (high)
Makes 6 servings

  1 pound ground turkey or chicken, or lean ground beef
  1 large onion, finely chopped
  1 large green sweet pepper, chopped
  1 16-ounce jar mild green salsa
  1 15- to 16-ounce can great Northern beans, rinsed and drained
  1 10-ounce bag romaine salad mix
  3 cups crushed tortilla chips
  ½ cup sliced green onions
  ½ cup chopped fresh cilantro
     Chopped tomato (optional)

1. In a large skillet, brown ground meat; drain fat. Transfer to a 3½- to 4-quart slow cooker. Stir in onion, sweet pepper, salsa, and beans.

2. Cover and cook on low-heat setting for 6 to 8 hours or on high-heat setting for 3 to 3½ hours.

3. Divide greens among 6 plates. Top with salsa mixture. Sprinkle with chips, green onions, and cilantro. If desired, top with chopped tomato

Per serving: 375 cal., 13 g total fat (2 g sat. fat), 60 mg chol., 475 mg sodium, 44 g carb., 9 g fiber, 22 g pro.

Chicken Stroganoff

Cream of mushroom soup laced with roasted garlic and meaty chicken chunks give a new spin to traditional stroganoff.

Mu Shu-Style Chicken

This slow cooker version of mu shu differs from the classic because it features chicken instead of pork, and is served in tortillas instead of thin pancakes.
Prep: 20 minutes
Cook: 6 to 7 hours (low) or 3 to 3½ hours (high)
Makes 4 servings

2½ to 3 pounds meaty chicken pieces (breast halves, thighs, and drumsticks), skinned
¼ teaspoon salt
⅛ teaspoon ground black pepper
½ cup water
¼ cup soy sauce
2 teaspoons toasted sesame oil
¾ teaspoon ground ginger
8 7- to 8-inch flour tortillas
½ cup bottled hoisin sauce
2 cups packaged shredded broccoli (broccoli slaw mix) or packaged shredded cabbage with carrot (coleslaw mix)

1. Place chicken pieces in a 3½- or 4-quart slow cooker. Sprinkle with salt and pepper. In a small bowl, stir together the water, soy sauce, sesame oil, and ginger. Pour over chicken in cooker.

2. Cover and cook on low-heat setting for 6 to 7 hours or on high-heat setting for 3 to 3½ hours.

3. Remove chicken, reserving cooking liquid. When cool enough to handle, remove chicken from bones; discard bones. Using two forks, pull chicken apart into shreds. Return chicken to cooker; heat through.

4. To serve, spread each tortilla with 1 tablespoon of the hoisin sauce. Using a slotted spoon, spoon shredded chicken just below centers of tortillas. Top with shredded broccoli. Fold bottom edge of each tortilla up and over filling. Fold in opposite sides; roll up from bottom.
Per serving: 520 cal., 18 g total fat (4 g sat. fat), 115 mg chol., 1,315 mg sodium, 44 g carb., 3 g fiber, 44 g pro.

Chicken Stroganoff

For an easy dinner party, serve this elegant dish with your favorite steamed vegetables, purchased dinner rolls, and an extra-special dessert from the bakery.
Prep: 20 minutes
Cook: 6 to 7 hours (low) or 3 to 3½ hours (high)
Makes 6 to 8 servings

2 pounds skinless, boneless chicken breast halves and/or thighs
1 cup chopped onion
1 4-ounce can (drained weight) sliced mushrooms, drained
2 10¾-ounce cans condensed cream of mushroom soup with roasted garlic
⅓ cup water
12 ounces dried wide egg noodles
1 8-ounce carton dairy sour cream
Freshly ground black pepper (optional)
Fresh thyme sprigs (optional)

1. Cut chicken into 1-inch pieces. In a 3½- or 4-quart slow cooker, combine chicken pieces, onion, and mushrooms. In a medium bowl, stir together mushroom soup and the water. Pour over chicken and vegetables.

2. Cover and cook on low-heat setting for 6 to 7 hours or on high-heat setting for 3 to 3½ hours.

3. Cook noodles according to package directions; drain well. Just before serving, stir sour cream into mixture in cooker. Serve over hot cooked noodles. If desired, sprinkle with pepper and garnish with thyme.
Per serving: 539 cal., 14 g total fat (6 g sat. fat), 156 mg chol., 850 mg sodium, 55 g carb., 3 g fiber, 57 g pro.

Easy Italian Chicken

Bottled **spaghetti sauce** makes this **chicken and cabbage combo** as easy to put together as it is to **enjoy.** Serve it over whatever type of **pasta** you like best.

Basil-Cream Chicken Thighs

Alfredo sauce joins forces with cream cheese to boost this luscious dish into a flavor category all its own.

Prep: 15 minutes
Cook: 6 to 7 hours (low) or 3 to 3½ hours (high)
Makes 6 servings

2½ pounds chicken thighs, skinned
¼ teaspoon ground black pepper
1 3-ounce package cream cheese, cubed
1 10-ounce container refrigerated Alfredo sauce
¼ cup water
1 teaspoon dried basil, crushed
1 16-ounce package loose-pack frozen broccoli, cauliflower, and carrots
   Hot cooked fettuccine

1. Place chicken thighs in a 3½- or 4-quart slow cooker. Sprinkle with pepper. Add cream cheese. In a small bowl, stir together Alfredo sauce, the water, and basil. Pour over mixture in cooker. Top with frozen vegetables.

2. Cover and cook on low-heat setting for 6 to 7 hours or on high-heat setting for 3 to 3½ hours.

3. Transfer chicken to a serving platter. Stir vegetable mixture. Serve over chicken and hot fettuccine.

Per serving: 456 cal., 24 g total fat (12 g sat. fat), 136 mg chol., 415 mg sodium, 27 g carb., 4 g fiber, 30 g pro.

Poultry Ps and Qs

Storing chicken and turkey properly is the key to delicious poultry dishes. When you buy fresh poultry, check the "sell by" date on the package. This is the last day the product should be sold. Store it in the coldest part of your refrigerator and it will stay fresh for 1 to 2 days longer. If the chicken or turkey is packaged in supermarket trays, you can refrigerate it in its original wrapping.

Easy Italian Chicken

It's important to skin chicken pieces that are cooked in the slow cooker. Why? As the skin cooks, it takes on an unpleasant rubbery texture and it adds lots of fat to the dish.

Prep: 20 minutes
Cook: 6 to 7 hours (low) or 3 to 3½ hours (high)
Makes 4 to 6 servings

½ of a medium head cabbage, cut into wedges (about 12 ounces)
1 medium onion, sliced and separated into rings
1 4½-ounce jar (drained weight) sliced mushrooms, drained
2 tablespoons quick-cooking tapioca
2 to 2½ pounds meaty chicken pieces (breast halves, thighs, and drumsticks), skinned
2 cups purchased meatless spaghetti sauce
   Grated Parmesan cheese
   Hot cooked pasta (optional)

1. In a 3½- to 6-quart slow cooker, combine cabbage wedges, onion, and mushrooms. Sprinkle tapioca over vegetables. Place chicken pieces on vegetables. Pour spaghetti sauce over chicken.

2. Cover and cook on low-heat setting for 6 to 7 hours or on high-heat setting for 3 to 3½ hours. Transfer to a serving platter. Sprinkle with Parmesan cheese. If desired, serve with hot cooked pasta.

Per serving: 300 cal., 9 g total fat (3 g sat. fat), 94 mg chol., 662 mg sodium, 24 g carb., 4 g fiber, 35 g pro.

Wild Rice and Chicken Soup

Three flavors of chicken combine to make this no-fuss dish in a bowl. Serve it with a hot loaf of bread or rolls to complete your meal.

Wild Rice and Chicken Soup

Prep: 20 minutes
Cook: 6 to 8 hours (low) or 3 to 4 hours (high)
Makes 8 to 10 servings

2½	cups chopped cooked chicken (about 12 ounces)
2	cups sliced fresh mushrooms
2	medium carrots, coarsely shredded
2	stalks celery, sliced
1	10¾-ounce can condensed cream of chicken or cream of mushroom soup
1	6-ounce package long grain and wild rice mix
5	cups chicken broth
5	cups water

1. In a 5- to 6-quart slow cooker, combine cooked chicken, mushrooms, carrots, celery, soup, uncooked rice, and the contents of the rice seasoning packet. Gradually stir in chicken broth and the water.

2. Cover; cook on low-heat setting for 6 to 8 hours or on high-heat setting for 3 to 4 hours.

Per serving: 221 cal., 7 g total fat (2 g sat. fat), 44 mg chol., 1,251 mg sodium, 23 g carb., 2 g fiber, 18 g pro.

Mulligatawny

Look for canned coconut milk in the baking aisle of the supermarket.

Prep: 25 minutes
Cook: 6 to 7 hours (low) or 3 to 3½ hours (high), plus 15 minutes on high
Makes 6 servings

1	tablespoon olive oil
1	pound boneless, skinless chicken thighs, cut into 1-inch pieces
2	cups chopped potato
1	medium Granny Smith apple, peeled and coarsely chopped
1	large onion, chopped
2	medium carrots, sliced
1	teaspoon finely shredded lime peel
1	tablespoon lime juice
1½	teaspoons curry powder
¼	teaspoon salt
2	14-ounce cans chicken broth
½	cup purchased unsweetened coconut milk
½	cup instant white rice

1. In a large skillet heat olive oil over medium-high heat. Brown chicken, half at a time, in hot oil. Drain off fat.

2. In a 3½- or 4-quart slow cooker combine chicken, potato, apple, onion, carrots, lime peel, lime juice, curry powder, and salt. Pour broth over all.

3. Cover and cook on low-heat setting for 6 to 7 hours or on high-heat setting for 3 to 3½ hours.

4. If using low-heat setting, turn to high-heat setting. Stir in coconut milk and uncooked rice. Cover and cook about 15 minutes or until rice is tender.

Per serving: 250 cal., 10 g total fat (4 g sat. fat), 62 mg chol., 701 mg sodium, 22 g carb., 2 g fiber, 18 g pro.

Chicken Chili

Brimming with tender **chicken** and white kidney beans, this **fiery chili** owes its bold flavor to a **zesty mix** of cumin, oregano, garlic, and **jalapeño** chile pepper.

Barbecue-Chutney Chicken

Bottled mango chutney adds a flavor wallop to this curry-seasoned chicken.

Prep: 15 minutes
Cook: 6 to 7 hours (low) or 3 to 3½ hours (high)
Makes 4 to 6 servings

- 1 medium onion, cut into wedges
- 3 pounds meaty chicken pieces (breast halves, thighs, and drumsticks), skinned
- ¼ teaspoon salt
- ⅛ teaspoon ground black pepper
- ½ cup mango chutney
- ⅔ cup bottled barbecue sauce
- 1 teaspoon curry powder
  Hot cooked rice

1. Place onion in a 3½- or 4-quart slow cooker. Add chicken pieces; sprinkle with salt and pepper. Snip any large pieces of chutney. In a small bowl, stir together chutney, barbecue sauce, and curry powder. Pour over mixture in cooker.

2. Cover and cook on low-heat setting for 6 to 7 hours or on high-heat setting for 3 to 3½ hours. Serve chicken and chutney mixture with hot cooked rice.

Per serving: 538 cal., 12 g total fat (3 g sat. fat), 138 mg chol., 647 mg sodium, 57 g carb., 2 g fiber, 48 g pro.

Chicken Chili

Does your supermarket bakery carry bread bowls? If it does, they are ideal for serving this awesome chili.

Prep: 25 minutes
Cook: 5 to 6 hours (low) or 2½ to 3 hours (high)
Makes 2 servings

  Nonstick cooking spray
- 8 ounces skinless, boneless chicken breast halves, cut into 1-inch pieces
- 1 15-ounce can white kidney (cannellini) or Great Northern beans, rinsed and drained
- 1¼ cups reduced-sodium chicken broth
- ¼ cup chopped onion
- ⅓ cup chopped green sweet pepper
- ½ of a small fresh jalapeño chile pepper, seeded and finely chopped (see tip, below)
- ¼ teaspoon ground cumin
- ¼ teaspoon dried oregano, crushed
- ⅛ teaspoon ground white pepper
- 1 clove garlic, minced
- 2 tablespoons chopped tomato (optional)
- 2 tablespoons sliced green onion (optional)
- 2 tablespoons shredded Monterey Jack cheese (1 ounce) (optional)

1. Lightly coat an unheated medium skillet with cooking spray. Preheat skillet over medium-high heat. Brown chicken in hot skillet; drain off fat.

2. In a 1½-quart slow cooker, combine chicken, drained beans, broth, onion, sweet pepper, chile pepper, cumin, oregano, white pepper, and garlic.

3. Cover and cook on low-heat setting for 5 to 6 hours or on high-heat setting for 2½ to 3 hours. If no heat setting is available, cook for 4 to 5 hours.

4. If desired, sprinkle individual servings with tomato, green onion, and cheese.

Per serving: 275 cal., 2 g total fat (0 g sat. fat), 66 mg chol., 750 mg sodium, 33 g carb., 11 g fiber, 40 g pro.

Chile Pepper Savvy

Because chile peppers contain volatile oils that can burn your skin and eyes, avoid direct contact with them as much as possible. When working with chile peppers, wear plastic or rubber gloves. If your bare hands do touch the peppers, wash your hands and nails well with soap and warm water.

These slow-simmered **chicken legs** are **comfort food** at its finest. Simmered in wine and seasoned with thyme and rosemary, they're the **perfect partner** for fluffy mashed potatoes.

Chicken and Vegetables with Herbs

Chicken and Vegetables with Herbs

While fresh pearl onions need to be blanched and peeled, you can skip those steps with the frozen ones.

Prep: 20 minutes
Cook: 7 to 8 hours (low) or 3½ to 4 hours (high)
Makes 4 servings

 8 ounces mushrooms, halved
 1 cup frozen pearl onions
 ¾ cup chicken broth
 ¼ cup dry red wine
 2 tablespoons tomato paste
 ½ teaspoon garlic salt
 ½ teaspoon dried rosemary, crushed
 ½ teaspoon dried thyme, crushed
 ¼ teaspoon ground black pepper
 1 bay leaf
 4 small chicken legs (drumstick-thigh portion; skinned) (2 to 2½ pounds total)
    Chicken broth (optional)
 2 tablespoons all-purpose flour
    Hot cooked mashed potatoes (optional)
    Fresh parsley sprigs (optional)

1. In a 5½- or 6-quart slow cooker, combine mushrooms and pearl onions. Stir in the ½ cup broth, the wine, tomato paste, garlic salt, rosemary, thyme, pepper, and bay leaf. Add chicken legs to cooker.

2. Cover and cook on low-heat setting for 7 to 8 hours or on high-heat setting for 3½ to 4 hours.

3. Using a slotted spoon, transfer chicken and vegetables to a serving platter. Discard bay leaf. Cover chicken and vegetables and keep warm.

4. For sauce, skim fat from cooking liquid. Measure 2 cups of the cooking liquid, adding additional chicken broth, if necessary, to equal 2 cups total liquid. Transfer liquid to a medium saucepan. In a small bowl, stir the remaining ¼ cup broth into the flour; stir into liquid in saucepan. Cook and stir until thickened and bubbly; cook and stir for 1 minute more. Spoon some of the sauce over chicken. Pass remaining sauce. If desired, serve with mashed potatoes and garnish with parsley.

Per serving: 304 cal., 9 g total fat (2 g sat. fat), 159 mg chol., 548 mg sodium, 9 g carb., 1 g fiber, 43 g pro.

Teriyaki Chicken with Orange Sauce

Prep: 15 minutes
Cook: 4 to 5 hours (low) or 2 to 2½ hours (high)
Makes 4 servings

 1 16-ounce package loose-pack frozen broccoli, baby carrots, and water chestnuts
 2 tablespoons quick-cooking tapioca
 1 pound skinless, boneless chicken breast halves or thighs, cut into 1-inch pieces
 ¾ cup chicken broth
 3 tablespoons orange marmalade
 2 tablespoons bottled teriyaki sauce
 1 teaspoon dry mustard
 ½ teaspoon ground ginger
    Hot cooked rice

1. Place frozen vegetables in a 3½- or 4-quart slow cooker. Sprinkle tapioca over vegetables. Stir to combine. Place chicken pieces on vegetable mixture.

2. For sauce, in a small bowl, combine broth, marmalade, teriyaki sauce, mustard, and ginger. Pour sauce over chicken pieces.

3. Cover and cook on low-heat setting for 4 to 5 hours or on high-heat setting for 2 to 2½ hours. Serve chicken mixture with hot cooked rice.

Per serving: 375 cal., 4 g total fat (1 g sat. fat), 79 mg chol., 790 mg sodium, 52 g carb., 4 g fiber, 30 g pro.

Mole with Chicken and Rice

In this chicken favorite, mole, a spicy sauce made with chiles and chocolate, is a treat for the taste buds.

Prep: 25 minutes
Cook: 9 to 11 hours (low) or 4½ to 5½ hours (high)
Makes 4 to 6 servings

1	14½-ounce can diced tomatoes, undrained
½	cup chopped onion
¼	cup slivered almonds, toasted
3	cloves garlic, quartered
2	canned jalapeño chile peppers, drained (see tip, page 77)
3	tablespoons unsweetened cocoa powder
3	tablespoons raisins
1	tablespoon sesame seeds
1	teaspoon sugar
¼	teaspoon salt
¼	teaspoon ground cinnamon
⅛	teaspoon ground nutmeg
⅛	teaspoon ground coriander
2	tablespoons quick-cooking tapioca
1	2½- to 3-pound broiler-fryer chicken, cut up and skinned
2	tablespoons slivered almonds, toasted
	Hot cooked rice

1. For mole, in a blender or food processor, combine undrained tomatoes, onion, the ¼ cup almonds, the garlic, chile peppers, cocoa powder, raisins, sesame seeds, sugar, salt, cinnamon, nutmeg, and coriander. Cover; blend or process until mixture is a coarse puree.

2. Place tapioca in a 3½- or 4-quart slow cooker. Add chicken; pour mole over chicken.

3. Cover and cook on low-heat setting for 9 to 11 hours or on high-heat setting for 4½ to 5½ hours.

4. Transfer chicken to a serving platter. Stir the sauce; pour sauce over chicken. Sprinkle with the 2 tablespoons almonds. Serve with hot cooked rice.

Per serving: 448 cal., 23 g total fat (5 g sat. fat), 99 mg chol., 586 mg sodium, 24 g carb., 4 g fiber, 36 g pro.

Chicken Tortilla Soup

There's no need to measure lots of herbs or spices for this soup. They're already in the chicken broth and Mexican-style tomatoes.

Prep: 15 minutes
Cook: 6 to 7 hours (low) or 3 to 3½ hours (high)
Makes 4 servings

2	14-ounce cans chicken broth with roasted garlic
1	14½-ounce can Mexican-style stewed tomatoes, undrained
2	cups shredded cooked chicken (about 10 ounces)
2	cups frozen (yellow, green, and red) peppers and onion stir-fry vegetables
1	cup tortilla chips
	Sliced fresh jalapeño chile peppers (optional) (see tip, page 77)

1. In a 3½- or 4-quart slow cooker, combine broth, undrained tomatoes, chicken, and frozen vegetables.

2. Cover and cook on low-heat setting for 6 to 7 hours or on high-heat setting for 3 to 3½ hours.

3. To serve, ladle soup into warm soup bowls and top with tortilla chips. If desired, top with chile peppers.

Per serving: 181 cal., 4 g total fat (1 g sat. fat), 36 mg chol., 1,383 mg sodium, 19 g carb., 1 g fiber, 18 g pro.

Chicken Tortilla Soup

Coq Au Vin Stew

Beefy onion soup mix and red wine combine with **chicken thighs,** mushrooms, and onions for a **stew** that's luscious and **comforting** on a cold winter's day.

Sweet and Smoky Chicken

Wondering what to do with the extra chipotle chile peppers? Pack them in a freezer container covered with the sauce from the can. Then seal, label, and freeze the chiles for up to 2 months. Thaw them in the refrigerator when you need them.

Prep: 15 minutes
Cook: 6 to 7 hours (low) or 3 to 3½ hours (high)
Makes 4 to 6 servings

2½ to 3 pounds meaty chicken pieces (breast halves, thighs, and drumsticks), skinned
¼ teaspoon salt
⅛ teaspoon ground black pepper
1 cup chicken broth
½ cup seedless raspberry jam
½ cup snipped dried apricots
1 to 2 canned chipotle chile peppers in adobo sauce, chopped, plus 1 tablespoon adobo sauce (see tip, page 77)
1 tablespoon quick-cooking tapioca, finely ground

1. Place chicken in a 3½- or 4-quart slow cooker. Sprinkle with salt and black pepper. For sauce, in a small bowl, stir together broth, raspberry jam, dried apricots, chile peppers and adobo sauce, and tapioca. Pour over chicken in cooker.

2. Cover and cook on low-heat setting for 6 to 7 hours or on high-heat setting for 3 to 3½ hours.

3. Transfer chicken to a serving platter. Serve sauce over chicken.

Per serving: 412 cal., 10 g total fat (3 g sat. fat), 115 mg chol., 549 mg sodium, 41 g carb., 2 g fiber, 38 g pro.

Coq Au Vin Stew

Soak up the flavorful broth with chunks of your favorite crusty bread.

Prep: 20 minutes
Cook: 5 to 6 hours (low) or 2½ to 3 hours (high)
Makes 4 servings

Nonstick cooking spray
3 pounds chicken thighs, skinned
1 envelope (½ of a 2.2-ounce package) beefy onion soup mix
1½ cups loose-pack frozen small whole onions
2 cups fresh mushrooms, quartered
½ cup dry red wine
Hot cooked mashed potatoes (optional)
Snipped fresh basil or parsley (optional)

1. Lightly coat an unheated large skillet with cooking spray. Preheat skillet over medium heat. Cook chicken thighs, several at a time, in the hot skillet until brown; drain off fat. Place chicken thighs in a 3½- or 4-quart slow cooker.

2. Sprinkle chicken thighs with dry soup mix. Add onions and mushrooms. Pour wine over all.

3. Cover and cook on low-heat setting for 5 to 6 hours or on high-heat setting for 2½ to 3 hours. Using a slotted spoon, remove chicken from slow cooker. Use a fork to remove chicken from the bone, shredding it into bite-size pieces. Discard bones. Return chicken to mixture in cooker. If desired, serve with hot mashed potatoes and sprinkle with basil.

Per serving: 305 cal., 8 g total fat (2 g sat. fat), 161 mg chol., 759 mg sodium, 12 g carb., 2 g fiber, 41 g pro.

Sloppy Chicken Pizza Joes

Everyone will love this vegetable-studded chicken takeoff on ground beef sloppy sandwiches.

Prep: 20 minutes
Cook: 6 to 8 hours (low) or 3 to 4 hours (high)
Broil: 1 minute
Makes 8 sandwiches

Nonstick cooking spray
3   pounds uncooked ground chicken
    or uncooked ground turkey
2   14-ounce jars pizza sauce
2   cups frozen loose-pack (yellow, green and
    red) peppers and onion stir-fry vegetables,
    thawed and chopped
8   hoagie rolls, split
8   slices mozzarella or provolone cheese
    (8 ounces)

1. Coat an unheated large skillet with cooking spray. Preheat skillet over medium-high heat. Add chicken to hot skillet; cook until no longer pink and cooked through.

2. In a 3½- or 4-quart slow cooker, stir together pizza sauce and chopped vegetables. Stir in cooked chicken.

3. Cover and cook on low-heat setting for 6 to 8 hours or on high-heat setting for 3 to 4 hours.

4. Preheat broiler. Arrange split rolls, cut sides up, on an unheated broiler pan. Broil 3 inches from the heat for 1 to 2 minutes or until toasted. Spoon chicken mixture onto toasted roll bottoms. Top with cheese and top halves of rolls.

Per serving: 641 cal., 24 g total fat (3 g sat. fat), 16 mg chol., 1,132 mg sodium, 58 g carb., 2 g fiber, 47 g pro.

Chicken Osso Buco

Prep: 45 minutes
Cook: 5 to 6 hours (low) or 2½ to 3 hours (high)
Makes 6 servings

2   tablespoons all-purpose flour
½   teaspoon salt
¼   teaspoon ground black pepper
12 medium chicken drumsticks, skinned
    (about 3 pounds total)
2   tablespoons olive oil
1   cup chopped carrot
1   cup chopped onion
1   cup chopped celery
6   cloves garlic, minced
2   tablespoons quick-cooking tapioca
1   8-ounce can tomato sauce
½   cup dry white wine or chicken broth
¼   cup chicken broth
1   teaspoon finely shredded lemon peel
1   tablespoon lemon juice
1   teaspoon dried thyme, crushed
3   cups dried penne pasta

1. Place flour, salt, and black pepper in a resealable plastic bag. Add chicken, a few pieces at time, shaking to coat. In a 10-inch skillet, brown chicken, half at a time, in hot oil over medium heat about 10 minutes or until golden, turning once.

2. In a 4- to 5-quart slow cooker, combine carrot, onion, celery, and garlic. Sprinkle with tapioca. Place chicken on top of vegetables. In a medium bowl, stir together tomato sauce, wine, broth, lemon peel, lemon juice, and thyme; pour over chicken in cooker.

3. Cover and cook on low-heat setting for 5 to 6 hours or on high-heat setting for 2½ to 3 hours.

4. Prepare pasta according to package directions. Drain well. Spoon chicken and sauce over pasta.

Per serving: 407 cal., 9 g total fat (2 g sat. fat), 98 mg chol., 529 mg sodium, 42 g carb., 3 g fiber, 33 g pro.

Chicken Osso Buco

Although classic Italian **osso buco** is made with **veal shanks,** this slow-cooker version is tasty proof that **chicken drumsticks** can be a first-rate **substitute.**

85
poultry and fish

Chicken with Sourdough-Mushroom Stuffing

If you like, use regular French bread instead.

Prep: 40 minutes
Cook: 4 to 5 hours (high)
Makes 8 servings

Nonstick cooking spray

2 tablespoons finely shredded lemon peel

1 tablespoon ground sage

1 tablespoon seasoned salt

1½ teaspoons freshly ground black pepper

8 small chicken legs (drumstick-thigh portion), skinned (about 5 pounds total)

¼ cup butter

4 cups quartered or sliced fresh cremini, baby portobello, shiitake, and/or button mushrooms

2 cloves garlic, thinly sliced

8 cups sourdough baguette cut into 1-inch cubes (12 to 14 ounces)

1 cup coarsely shredded carrot

1 cup chicken broth

¼ cup chopped walnuts, toasted

¼ cup snipped fresh flat-leaf parsley

1. Lightly coat a 6-quart slow cooker with nonstick cooking spray. Set aside 1 teaspoon of the lemon peel. In a small bowl, combine the remaining 5 teaspoons lemon peel, the sage, seasoned salt, and pepper. Remove three-fourths of the sage mixture; sprinkle on the chicken legs and rub in with your fingers. Place chicken legs in the cooker.

2. Meanwhile, in a large skillet, melt butter over medium heat. Add mushrooms and garlic; cook and stir for 3 to 5 minutes or just until tender. Stir in remaining sage mixture. In a large bowl, combine bread cubes and carrot; add mushroom mixture. Drizzle with chicken broth; toss gently. Lightly pack stuffing on top of chicken in cooker. Cover and cook on high-heat setting for 4 to 5 hours.

3. Using a slotted spoon, transfer stuffing and chicken to a serving platter; discard juices in cooker. In a small bowl, combine the reserved 1 teaspoon lemon peel, walnuts, and parsley; sprinkle on chicken.

Per serving: 412 cal., 17 g total fat (5 g sat. fat), 146 mg chol., 1,450 mg sodium, 27 g carb., 3 g fiber, 39 g pro.

Fennel and Pear Chicken Thighs

Prep: 20 minutes
Cook: 7 to 8 hours (low) or 3½ to 4 hours (high)
Makes 6 servings

1 medium fennel bulb, trimmed and cut into ½-inch-thick wedges

2 6- to 7-ounce jars (drained weight) sliced mushrooms, drained

½ cup coarsely snipped dried pears

2 tablespoons quick-cooking tapioca, finely ground

2½ pounds skinless, boneless chicken thighs

¾ teaspoon salt

½ teaspoon dried thyme, crushed

½ teaspoon cracked black pepper

1 cup pear nectar or apple juice

Hot cooked couscous or rice

Fennel tops (optional)

1. In a 3½- or 4-quart slow cooker, combine sliced fennel, mushrooms, and dried pears. Sprinkle with tapioca. Add chicken thighs; sprinkle with salt, thyme, and pepper. Pour pear nectar over mixture in cooker.

2. Cover and cook on low-heat setting for 7 to 8 hours or on high-heat setting for 3½ to 4 hours. Serve chicken mixture with hot cooked couscous. If desired, garnish with fennel tops.

Per serving: 407 cal., 7 g total fat (2 g sat. fat), 157 mg chol., 657 mg sodium, 41 g carb., 4 g fiber, 42 g pro.

Fennel and Pear Chicken Thighs

The licoricelike flavor of **fennel** tastes terrific with the **pears** in this family pleasing dish. Because the pears are **dried** rather than **fresh,** you can make this recipe any **time of year.**

Turkey Shepherd's Pie

Traditionally made with lamb or mutton, shepherd's pie is equally tasty when slow-cooked with turkey.

Prep: 20 minutes
Cook: 6 to 7 hours (low) or 3 to 3½ hours (high), plus 10 minutes on high
Makes 4 servings

12 ounces turkey breast tenderloin or skinless, boneless chicken breast halves
 1 10-ounce package frozen mixed vegetables
 1 12-ounce jar turkey or chicken gravy
 1 teaspoon dried thyme, crushed
 1 20-ounce package refrigerated mashed potatoes

1. Cut turkey into ½-inch-wide strips. Place frozen vegetables in a 3½- or 4-quart slow cooker. Top with turkey strips. In a small bowl, stir together gravy and thyme; pour over turkey.

2. Cover and cook on low-heat setting for 6 to 7 hours or on high-heat setting for 3 to 3½ hours.

3. If using low-heat setting, turn to high-heat setting. Using a spoon, drop mashed potatoes into eight mounds on top of turkey mixture. Cover and cook for 10 minutes more. To serve, spoon some of the turkey mixture and two of the potato mounds into each of four shallow bowls.

Per serving: 297 cal., 5 g total fat (1 g sat. fat), 51 mg chol., 781 mg sodium, 33 g carb., 4 g fiber, 27 g pro.

Chicken and Vegetable Bean Soup

When there's no leftover cooked chicken in the fridge, pick up a roasted bird at your supermarket's deli section.

Prep: 15 minutes
Stand: 1 hour
Cook: 8 to 10 hours (low) or 4 to 5 hours (high), plus 30 minutes on high
Makes 4 to 6 servings

 1 cup dry Great Northern beans
 6 cups water
 1 cup chopped onion
 1 medium fennel bulb, trimmed and cut into ½-inch pieces
 2 medium carrots, chopped
 2 cloves garlic, minced
 2 tablespoons snipped fresh parsley
 1 teaspoon dried rosemary, crushed
 ¼ teaspoon ground black pepper
 4½ cups chicken broth
 2½ cups shredded or chopped cooked chicken
 1 14½-ounce can diced tomatoes, undrained

1. Rinse beans; drain. In a large saucepan, combine beans and the water. Bring to boiling; reduce heat. Simmer, uncovered, for 10 minutes. Remove from heat. Cover and let stand for 1 hour. Drain and rinse beans.

2. Meanwhile, in a 3½- to 5-quart slow cooker, combine onion, fennel, carrots, garlic, parsley, rosemary, and pepper. Place beans on top of vegetables in cooker. Pour broth over all.

3. Cover and cook on low-heat setting for 8 to 10 hours or on high-heat setting for 4 to 5 hours.

4. If using low-heat setting, turn to high-heat setting. Stir in chicken and undrained tomatoes. Cover and cook about 30 minutes more or until heated through.

Per serving: 426 cal., 10 g total fat (3 g sat. fat), 78 mg chol., 1,454 mg sodium, 46 g carb., 15 g fiber, 40 g pro.

Chicken and Vegetable Bean Soup

This **chicken soup** is a notch above the rest. It's a captivating mix of Great Northern **beans,** fennel, carrots, and **tomatoes**—all simmered with **rosemary,** parsley, and garlic.

Asian Turkey and Rice Soup

Slices of mushrooms, slivers of bok choy, and chunks of turkey mingle in a soy- and ginger-flavored broth, giving stir-fry flavors to this savory soup.

Prep: 25 minutes
Cook: 7 to 8 hours (low) or 3½ to 4 hours (high), plus 10 minutes on high
Makes 6 servings

2	14-ounce cans reduced-sodium chicken broth
1	pound turkey breast tenderloin or skinless, boneless chicken breast halves, cut into 1-inch pieces
2	cups sliced fresh mushrooms (such as shiitake or button)
1½	cups water
2	medium carrots, peeled and cut into thin, bite-size strips
½	cup chopped onion
2	tablespoons reduced-sodium soy sauce
2	teaspoons grated fresh ginger
4	cloves garlic, minced
1½	cups sliced bok choy
1	cup instant brown rice

1. In a 3½- or 4-quart slow cooker, combine broth, turkey, mushrooms, the water, carrots, onion, soy sauce, ginger, and garlic.

2. Cover and cook on low-heat setting for 7 to 8 hours or on high-heat setting for 3½ to 4 hours.

3. If using low-heat setting, turn to high-heat setting. Stir in bok choy and uncooked rice. Cover and cook for 10 to 15 minutes more or until rice is tender.

Per serving: 166 cal., 2 g total fat (0 g sat. fat), 45 mg chol., 572 mg sodium, 15 g carb., 2 g fiber, 22 g pro.

Sesame-Ginger Turkey Wraps

If you're not feeding a crowd, refrigerate or freeze the leftover turkey to reheat for another meal.

Prep: 20 minutes
Cook: 6 to 7 hours (low) or 3 to 3½ hours (high)
Stand: 5 minutes
Makes 12 servings

	Nonstick cooking spray
3	turkey thighs, skinned (3½ to 4 pounds total)
1	cup bottled sesame-ginger stir-fry sauce
¼	cup water
1	16-ounce package shredded broccoli (broccoli slaw mix)
12	8-inch flour tortillas, warmed*
¾	cup sliced green onions

1. Lightly coat a 3½- or 4-quart slow cooker with cooking spray. Place turkey thighs in prepared cooker. In a small bowl, stir together stir-fry sauce and the water. Pour over turkey in cooker.

2. Cover and cook on low-heat setting for 6 to 7 hours or on high-heat setting for 3 to 3½ hours.

3. Remove turkey from cooker; cool slightly. Remove turkey from bones; discard bones. Using two forks, shred turkey into bite-size pieces. Return to mixture in cooker. Place broccoli slaw mix in sauce mixture in the cooker. Stir to coat; cover and let stand for 5 minutes. Using a slotted spoon, remove turkey and broccoli from cooker.

4. To assemble, place some of the turkey mixture on each warmed tortilla. Top turkey mixture with green onions. If desired, spoon some of the sauce from cooker on top of green onions. Roll up and serve immediately.

Per serving: 207 cal., 5 g total fat (1 g sat. fat), 67 mg chol., 422 mg sodium, 20 g carb., 2 g fiber, 20 g pro.

*Note: To warm tortillas, preheat oven to 350°F. Stack tortillas and wrap tightly in foil. Heat in the oven about 10 minutes or until heated through.

Sesame-Ginger Turkey Wraps

Turkey and Pasta Primavera

Turkey-Vegetable Goulash

This goulash recipe saves time and dishwashing by cooking the noodles in the slow cooker.

Prep: 20 minutes
Cook: 6 to 8 hours (low) or 3 to 4 hours (high), plus 20 minutes on high
Makes 6 servings

- 1   **pound uncooked ground turkey**
- 1   **14½-ounce can diced tomatoes with basil, oregano, and garlic, undrained**
- 1   **10-ounce package frozen mixed vegetables**
- 1½   **cups water**
- 1   **8-ounce can tomato sauce**
- 2   **stalks celery, sliced**
- 1   **small onion, chopped**
- 1   **0.9-ounce envelope turkey gravy mix**
- 1   **cup dried fine egg noodles**
- ⅓   **cup shredded sharp cheddar, Monterey Jack, or Parmesan cheese**

1. In a large skillet, cook ground turkey until brown. Drain off fat. Transfer turkey to a 3½- or 4-quart slow cooker. Stir in undrained tomatoes, frozen vegetables, the water, tomato sauce, celery, onion, and dry gravy mix.

2. Cover and cook on low-heat setting for 6 to 8 hours or on high-heat setting for 3 to 4 hours.

3. If using low-heat setting, turn to high-heat setting. Stir in uncooked noodles. Cover and cook for 20 to 30 minutes more or until noodles are tender. Sprinkle with cheese.

Per serving: 251 cal., 9 g total fat (3 g sat. fat), 73 mg chol., 918 mg sodium, 22 g carb., 3 g fiber, 19 g pro.

Turkey and Pasta Primavera

A sprinkling of Parmesan cheese brings a tantalizing accent to a creamy blend of turkey, pasta, and veggies.

Prep: 15 minutes
Cook: 4 to 5 hours (low) or 2 to 2½ hours (high)
Makes 8 servings

- 2   **pounds turkey breast tenderloins or skinless, boneless chicken breast halves, cut into 1-inch pieces**
- 1   **16-ounce package frozen loose-pack stir-fry vegetables (sugar snap peas, carrots, onions, and mushrooms)**
- 2   **teaspoons dried basil, oregano, or Italian seasoning, crushed**
- 1   **16-ounce jar Alfredo pasta sauce**
- 12   **ounces dried linguine or spaghetti, broken**
      Shredded Parmesan cheese (optional)

1. In a 4½- to 6-quart slow cooker, combine turkey and frozen vegetables. Sprinkle with dried herb. Stir in Alfredo sauce.

2. Cover and cook on low-heat setting for 4 to 5 hours or on high-heat setting for 2 to 2½ hours.

3. Cook pasta according to package directions; drain. Stir pasta into mixture in slow cooker. If desired, sprinkle individual servings with Parmesan cheese.

Per serving: 488 cal., 19 g total fat (0 g sat. fat), 99 mg chol., 267 mg sodium, 39 g carb., 3 g fiber, 37 g pro.

Two for One

Many slow-cooker main dishes make enough servings that you will have enough for another meal. Cool the leftovers slightly and transfer them to a freezer container. Label and freeze them for up to 6 months. To serve, thaw the leftovers in the refrigerator and reheat them on the stove top or in a microwave oven, stirring several times.

Cajun Shrimp and Rice

Cajun Shrimp and Rice

Assemble the ingredients in the slow cooker and set an electric timer to start the cooker while you're away. Add the chilled shrimp and let it heat while you set the table and toss a salad.

Prep: 20 minutes
Cook: 5 to 6 hours (low) or 3 to 3½ hours (high), plus 15 minutes on high
Makes 6 servings

1	28-ounce can tomatoes, cut up, undrained
1	14-ounce can chicken broth
1	cup chopped onion
1	cup chopped green sweet pepper
1	6- to 6¼-ounce package long-grain and wild rice mix
¼	cup water
2	cloves garlic, minced
½	teaspoon Cajun seasoning
1	pound cooked, peeled, and deveined shrimp
	Bottled hot pepper sauce (optional)

1. In a 3½- or 4-quart slow cooker combine undrained tomatoes, broth, onion, sweet pepper, rice mix with seasoning packet, water, garlic, and Cajun seasoning.

2. Cover; cook on low-heat setting for 5 to 6 hours or on high-heat setting for 3 to 3½ hours.

3. If using low-heat setting, turn slow cooker to high-heat setting. Stir shrimp into rice mixture. Cover; cook for 15 minutes more. If desired, pass hot pepper sauce.

Per serving: 223 cal., 2 g total fat (0 g sat. fat), 147 mg chol., 1,063 mg sodium, 32 g carb., 3 g fiber, 21 g pro.

Creamed Turkey and Smoked Salmon

A downhome favorite goes uptown! Smoked salmon and dillweed add a gourmet angle to creamed turkey and mushrooms.

Prep: 15 minutes
Cook: 3½ hours (low) or 1½ hours (high), plus 15 minutes on high
Makes 6 servings

2	pounds turkey breast tenderloins
8	ounces fresh mushrooms, quartered
⅓	cup water
1	teaspoon salt
½	teaspoon dried dillweed, crushed
¼	teaspoon black pepper
¾	cup fat-free half-and-half
2	tablespoons cornstarch
4	ounces smoked salmon (not lox-style), skinned and flaked
¼	cup sliced green onions (2)

1. Cut turkey into 1-inch pieces. In a 3½- or 4-quart slow cooker combine turkey and mushrooms. Stir in water, salt, dillweed, and pepper.

2. Cover and cook on low-heat setting for 3½ hours or on high-heat setting for 1½ hours.

3. If using low-heat setting, turn to high-heat setting. In a small bowl combine half-and-half and cornstarch. Stir into mixture in cooker. Cover and cook for 15 minutes more. Stir in salmon and green onions.

Per serving: 227 cal., 2 g total fat (0 g sat. fat), 104 mg chol., 628 mg sodium, 7 g carb., 0 g fiber, 42 g pro.

Manhattan-Style Clam Chowder

Tomatoes and tomato juice make this New York-style chowder stand apart from its creamy New England cousin. To save prep time, skip peeling the potatoes.

Prep: 20 minutes
Cook: 8 to 10 hours (low) or 4 to 5 hours (high), plus 5 minutes on high
Makes 4 servings

- 2 6½-ounce cans minced clams or one 10-ounce can baby clams
- 2 medium potatoes, peeled and cut into ½-inch cubes
- 1 cup chopped onion
- 1 cup chopped celery with leaves
- ½ cup chopped green sweet pepper
- 1 14½-ounce can Italian-style stewed tomatoes, undrained
- 1½ cups hot-style tomato juice or hot-style vegetable juice
- ½ teaspoon dried thyme, crushed
- 1 bay leaf
- 4 slices bacon, crisp-cooked, drained, and crumbled, or ¼ cup cooked bacon pieces

1. Drain clams, reserving liquid (about ⅔ cup liquid). Place clams in a small bowl; cover and chill.

2. In a 3½- or 4-quart slow cooker, combine reserved clam liquid, potatoes, onion, celery, and sweet pepper; stir in undrained tomatoes, tomato juice, thyme, and bay leaf.

3. Cover and cook on low-heat setting for 8 to 10 hours or on high-heat setting for 4 to 5 hours.

4. If using low-heat setting, turn to high-heat setting. Stir in chilled clams. Cover and cook on high-heat setting for 5 minutes more. Discard bay leaf. Sprinkle individual servings with bacon.

Per serving: 238 cal., 5 g total fat (1 g sat. fat), 34 mg chol., 719 mg sodium, 30 g carb., 4 g fiber, 17 g pro.

Mexican-Style Fish Chowder

Chunks of cod get a flavorful kick from seasoned tomatoes in this zesty chowder. Serve it with blue tortilla chips and Mexican beer.

Prep: 15 minutes
Cook: 3 to 4 hours (low) or 1½ to 2 hours (high), plus 1 hour on high
Makes 6 to 8 servings

- Nonstick cooking spray
- 2 10¾-ounce cans condensed cream of celery soup
- 1 16- to 20-ounce package frozen whole kernel corn
- 1½ cups milk
- 1 pound fresh or frozen cod or other white-flesh fish fillets
- 2 14½-ounce cans Mexican-style stewed tomatoes, undrained

1. Lightly coat a 3½- or 4-quart slow cooker with cooking spray. In the prepared cooker, combine cream of celery soup, corn, and milk.

2. Cover and cook on low-heat setting for 3 to 4 hours or on high-heat setting for 1½ to 2 hours.

3. Meanwhile, thaw fish, if frozen. Rinse fish; pat dry with paper towels. If using low-heat setting, turn to high-heat setting. Stir chowder. Place fish on top of the mixture in the cooker. Cover and cook for 1 hour more. Stir in undrained tomatoes.

Per serving: 293 cal., 8 g total fat (3 g sat. fat), 39 mg chol., 1,296 mg sodium, 36 g carb., 2 g fiber, 21 g pro.

Hearty Fish Chowder

This thick and chunky fish soup measures up to the finest chowders anywhere. If you prefer halibut or haddock, substitute either for the cod.

Prep: 25 minutes
Cook: 6 to 7 hours (low) or 3 to 3½ hours (high), plus 1 hour on high
Makes 6 servings

Hearty Fish Chowder

2	medium potatoes, chopped (2 cups)
1	cup chopped onion
2	cloves garlic, minced
1	10¾-ounce can condensed cream of celery soup
1	10-ounce package frozen whole kernel corn
1	10-ounce package frozen baby lima beans or 2 cups loose-pack frozen baby lima beans
1½	cups chicken broth
⅓	cup dry white wine or chicken broth
1	teaspoon lemon-pepper seasoning
1	pound fresh or frozen cod or other whitefish fillets
1	14½-ounce can stewed tomatoes, undrained
⅓	cup nonfat dry milk powder

1. In a 3½- or 4-quart slow cooker, combine potatoes, onion, garlic, soup, corn, lima beans, broth, white wine, and lemon-pepper seasoning.

2. Cover and cook on low-heat setting for 6 to 7 hours or on high-heat setting for 3 to 3½ hours.

3. Meanwhile, thaw fish, if frozen. Rinse fish; pat dry with paper towels. Place fish on the mixture in the cooker. If using low-heat setting, turn to high-heat setting. Cover and cook for 1 hour more.

4. Add undrained tomatoes and nonfat dry milk powder to cooker, stirring gently to break up the fish.

Per serving: 317 cal., 4 g total fat (1 g sat. fat), 40 mg chol., 1,034 mg sodium, 45 g carb., 6 g fiber, 24 g pro.

Vegetable Stew with Cornmeal Dumplings

meatless favorites

Whether you prepare meatless meals on a regular basis or simply enjoy them as a change of pace, these creative meat-free dishes will add delicious variety to your menus. Choose from soups and stews, casseroles, pasta dishes, and more.

Vegetable Stew with Cornmeal Dumplings

The hint of Parmesan cheese in the cornmeal dumplings makes them a fine match for this Italian-seasoned stew.

Prep: 25 minutes   **Cook:** 8 to 10 hours (low) or 4 to 5 hours (high), plus 50 minutes on high

Makes 6 servings

3   cups peeled butternut or acorn squash cut into $\frac{1}{2}$-inch cubes

2   cups sliced fresh mushrooms

2   14$\frac{1}{2}$-ounce cans diced tomatoes, undrained

1   15-ounce can Great Northern beans, rinsed and drained

1   cup water

4   cloves garlic, minced

1   teaspoon dried Italian seasoning, crushed

$\frac{1}{4}$ teaspoon ground black pepper

$\frac{1}{2}$ cup all-purpose flour

$\frac{1}{3}$ cup cornmeal

2   tablespoons grated Parmesan cheese

1   tablespoon snipped fresh parsley

1   teaspoon baking powder

$\frac{1}{4}$ teaspoon salt

1   egg

2   tablespoons milk

2   tablespoons cooking oil

1   9-ounce package frozen Italian green beans or frozen cut green beans
    Paprika

1. In a 3$\frac{1}{2}$- or 4-quart slow cooker, combine squash, mushrooms, undrained tomatoes, Great Northern beans, the water, garlic, Italian seasoning, and pepper.

2. Cover and cook on low-heat setting for 8 to 10 hours or on high-heat setting for 4 to 5 hours.

3. For dumplings: In a medium bowl, stir together flour, cornmeal, Parmesan cheese, parsley, baking powder, and salt. In a small bowl, whisk together egg, milk, and oil. Add to the flour mixture; stir with a fork just until combined.

4. If using low-heat setting, turn to high-heat setting. Stir frozen green beans into stew. Drop the dumpling dough into six mounds on top of the stew. Sprinkle with paprika. Cover and cook for 50 minutes more. (Do not lift lid while dumplings are cooking.)

Per serving: 288 cal., 7 g total fat (2 g sat. fat), 37 mg chol., 442 mg sodium, 45 g carb., 7 g fiber, 12 g pro.

Vegetable-Rice Casserole

Toss a salad to serve with this cheesy garbanzo and veggie combo and dinner is ready.

Prep: 15 minutes
Cook: 3½ to 4½ hours (low)
Makes 4 servings

- 1 **16-ounce package frozen loose-pack cauliflower, broccoli, and carrots**
- 1 **15-ounce can garbanzo beans (chickpeas), rinsed and drained**
- 1 **10¾-ounce can condensed cream of celery or cream of mushroom soup**
- 1 **cup instant white rice**
- ½ **of a 15-ounce jar (about 1 cup) processed cheese dip**
- 1 **cup water**

1. In a 3½- or 4-quart slow cooker, combine frozen vegetables and drained beans. In a medium bowl, combine cream of celery soup, uncooked rice, cheese dip, and the water. Pour over the vegetables in cooker.

2. Cover and cook on low-heat setting for 3½ to 4½ hours or until vegetables and rice are tender. Stir well before serving.

Per serving: 436 cal., 17 g total fat (10 g sat. fat), 34 mg chol., 1,923 mg sodium, 52 g carb., 9 g fiber, 17 g pro.

Creamy Tortellini Soup

White sauce mix and dried tortellini make this satisfying soup extra easy; stirring in the spinach at the last minute gives it fresh-from-the garden flavor.

Prep: 20 minutes
Cook: 5 to 6 hours (low), plus 1 hour, or 2½ to 3 hours (high), plus 45 minutes
Makes 4 servings

- 1 **1.8-ounce envelope white sauce mix**
- 4 **cups water**
- 1 **14-ounce can vegetable broth**
- 1½ **cups sliced fresh mushrooms**
- ½ **cup chopped onion**
- 3 **cloves garlic, minced**
- ½ **teaspoon dried basil, crushed**
- ¼ **teaspoon salt**
- ¼ **teaspoon dried oregano, crushed**
- ⅛ **teaspoon cayenne pepper**
- 1 **7- to 8-ounce package dried cheese tortellini (about 2 cups)**
- 1 **12-ounce can evaporated milk**
- 6 **cups fresh baby spinach leaves or torn spinach**
  Ground black pepper (optional)
  Finely shredded Parmesan cheese (optional)

1. Place dry white sauce mix in a 3½- or 4-quart slow cooker. Gradually add the water to the white sauce mix, stirring until smooth. Stir in broth, mushrooms, onion, garlic, basil, salt, oregano, and cayenne pepper.

2. Cover and cook on low-heat setting for 5 to 6 hours or on high-heat setting for 2½ to 3 hours.

3. Stir in dried tortellini. Cover and cook on low-heat setting for 1 hour more or high-heat setting for 45 minutes more.

4. Stir in evaporated milk and spinach. If desired, sprinkle individual servings with black pepper and Parmesan cheese.

Per serving: 450 cal., 18 g total fat (7 g sat. fat), 34 mg chol., 1,710 mg sodium, 53 g carb., 2 g fiber, 22 g pro.

Creamy Tortellini Soup

Vegetable Chili

Garlic-Artichoke Pasta

Seasoned tomatoes blend with garlic, artichokes, and cream for a sensational sauce to serve over any favorite pasta. The olives and feta cheese sprinkled on top add a Mediterranean touch.

Prep: 15 minutes
Cook: 6 to 8 hours (low) or 3 to 4 hours (high)
Stand: 5 minutes
Makes 6 servings

　　Nonstick cooking spray
3　14½-ounce cans diced tomatoes with basil, oregano, and garlic, undrained
2　14-ounce cans artichoke hearts, drained and quartered
6　cloves garlic, minced
½　cup whipping cream
12　ounces dried linguine, fettuccine, or other favorite pasta
　　Sliced pimiento-stuffed green olives and/or sliced pitted ripe olives (optional)
　　Crumbled feta cheese or finely shredded Parmesan cheese (optional)

1. Coat a 3½- or 4-quart slow cooker with cooking spray. Drain two of the cans of diced tomatoes (do not drain remaining can). In the prepared cooker, combine drained and undrained tomatoes, drained artichoke hearts, and garlic.

2. Cover and cook on low-heat setting for 6 to 8 hours or on high-heat setting for 3 to 4 hours.

3. Stir in whipping cream; let stand about 5 minutes to heat through.

4. Meanwhile, cook pasta according to package directions; drain. Serve sauce over hot cooked pasta. If desired, top with olives and/or feta cheese.

Per serving: 403 cal., 8 g total fat (5 g sat. fat), 27 mg chol., 1,513 mg sodium, 68 g carb., 7 g fiber, 13 g pro.

Vegetable Chili

This hearty chili for two features black beans and a multitude of vegetables.

Prep: 20 minutes
Cook: 6 to 8 hours (low) or 3 to 4 hours (high)
Makes 2 servings

1　15-ounce can black beans, rinsed and drained
1½　cups low-sodium tomato juice
1　cup loose-pack frozen whole kernel corn
¾　cup coarsely chopped zucchini or yellow summer squash
⅓　cup coarsely chopped red or yellow sweet pepper
¼　cup chopped onion
1　teaspoon chili powder
¼　teaspoon dried oregano, crushed
⅛　teaspoon salt
1　clove garlic, minced

1. In a 1½-quart slow cooker, combine drained beans, tomato juice, corn, zucchini, sweet pepper, onion, chili powder, oregano, salt, and garlic.

2. Cover and cook on low-heat setting for 6 to 8 hours or on high-heat setting for 3 to 4 hours. If no heat setting is available, cook for 5 to 6 hours.

Per serving: 271 cal., 2 g total fat (0 g sat. fat), 0 mg chol., 790 mg sodium, 59 g carb., 14 g fiber, 19 g pro.

Sweet and Sour Cabbage Rolls

Raisins and brown sugar **sweeten** purchased marinara **sauce** while a splash of lemon juice adds a **pleasing tartness** to this recipe.

Sweet and Sour Cabbage Rolls

Prep: 1 hour
Cook: 7 to 9 hours (low) or 3½ to 4½ hours (high)
Makes 4 servings

 1   large head green cabbage
 1   15-ounce can black beans or red kidney beans, rinsed and drained
 1   cup cooked brown rice
 ½   cup chopped carrots
 ½   cup chopped celery
 1   medium onion, chopped
 1   clove garlic, minced
 3½ cups marinara sauce
 ⅓   cup raisins
 3   tablespoons lemon juice
 1   tablespoon brown sugar

1. Remove 8 large outer leaves from head of cabbage. In a Dutch oven cook cabbage leaves in boiling water for 4 to 5 minutes or just until leaves are limp; drain. Trim the thick rib in center of each leaf. Set leaves aside. Shred 4 cups of the remaining cabbage and place in a 3½- to 6-quart slow cooker.

2. In medium bowl combine beans, cooked rice, carrots, celery, onion, garlic, and ½ cup of the marinara sauce. Divide bean mixture evenly among the 8 cabbage leaves, using about ⅓ cup per leaf. Fold sides of leaf over filling and roll up. Repeat with remaining cabbage rolls

3. Combine remaining marinara sauce, raisins, lemon juice, and brown sugar. Pour half of the sauce mixture over shredded cabbage in cooker; stir. Place cabbage rolls on top of shredded cabbage. Top with sauce.

4. Cover and cook on low-heat setting for 7 to 9 hours or on high-heat setting for 3½ to 4½ hours. Carefully remove the cooked cabbage rolls and serve with the shredded cabbage.

Per serving: 406 cal., 12 g total fat (3 g sat. fat), 0 mg chol., 1,476 mg sodium, 69 g carb., 15 g fiber, 14 g pro.

Pinto Bean and Couscous Tostadas

Beef or chicken broth will also work well in this meatless south-of-the-border entrée.

Prep: 25 minutes
Cook: 8 to 10 hours (low) or 4 to 5 hours (high)
Stand: 1 hour plus 5 minutes
Makes 8 servings

 1½ cups dry pinto beans
 2   cups water
 1   14-ounce can vegetable broth
 1   cup chopped carrots
 ¼   teaspoon salt
 ¼   teaspoon crushed red pepper
 1   cup purchased salsa
 1   cup quick-cooking couscous
 8   tostada shells
     Shredded cheddar cheese
     Dairy sour cream, shredded lettuce, and/or purchased salsa (optional)

1. Rinse beans; place in a large saucepan. Add enough water to cover beans by 2 inches. Bring to boiling; reduce heat. Simmer, uncovered, for 10 minutes. Remove from heat. Cover and let stand for 1 hour. Drain and rinse beans.

2. In a 3½- or 4-quart slow cooker stir together beans, the 2 cups water, broth, carrots, salt, and crushed red pepper.

3. Cover and cook on low-heat setting for 8 to 10 hours or on high-heat setting for 4 to 5 hours.

4. Stir in the 1 cup salsa and the uncooked couscous. Remove liner from slow cooker, if possible, or turn off slow cooker. Let stand, covered, for 5 minutes. Serve bean-couscous mixture on tostada shells; top with cheese. If desired, serve with sour cream, lettuce, and/or additional salsa.

Per serving: 304 cal., 6 g total fat (2 g sat. fat), 9 mg chol., 477 mg sodium, 49 g carb., 8 g fiber, 13 g pro.

Cuban-Style Black Beans and Rice

Beans and rice are a favorite combination worldwide. In this lively Cuban version, garlic, lime peel, and jalapeño pepper spice up the black beans.

Prep: 20 minutes
Stand: 1 hour
Cook: 10 to 12 hours (low) or 5 to 6 hours (high)
Makes 5 servings

4	cups water
1½	cups dry black beans, rinsed and drained
2	14-ounce cans reduced-sodium chicken broth
1	cup chopped onion
2	bay leaves
1	to 2 fresh jalapeño chile peppers, seeded and finely chopped (see tip, page 77)
4	cloves garlic, minced
2	teaspoons ground cumin
2	teaspoons finely shredded lime peel
¾	teaspoon salt
¼	teaspoon ground black pepper
	Hot cooked brown rice
	Snipped fresh cilantro (optional)
	Chopped fresh jalapeño chile peppers (optional) (see tip, page 77)
	Chopped tomatoes (optional)
	Chopped onion (optional)
	Lime wedges (optional)

1. In a large saucepan, combine the 4 cups water and the beans. Bring to boiling; reduce heat. Simmer, uncovered, for 10 minutes. Remove from heat. Cover and let stand for 1 hour. Drain and rinse beans.

2. Place beans in a 3½- or 4-quart slow cooker. Add broth, the 1 cup chopped onion, the bay leaves, finely chopped chile peppers, garlic, cumin, lime peel, salt, and black pepper.

3. Cover and cook on low-heat setting for 10 to 12 hours or on high-heat setting for 5 to 6 hours.

4. Discard bay leaves. Mash beans slightly. Serve beans with hot cooked rice. If desired, garnish with cilantro, chopped chile peppers, tomatoes, additional chopped onion, and lime wedges.

Per serving: 353 cal., 2 g total fat (0 g sat. fat), 0 mg chol., 795 mg sodium, 67 g carb., 12 g fiber, 18 g pro.

Keep Tabs on Salt

Extra sodium in your diet may increase your blood pressure, which can be dangerous to your health. To reduce the salt in dishes that include canned beans, such as Cuban-Style Black Beans and Rice, drain the beans in a colander. Then rinse them under cold water to remove some of the salty liquid.

Cuban-Style Black Beans and Rice

Savory Bean and Spinach Soup

Savory Bean and Spinach Soup

Just like Goldilocks, you'll find the converted rice is "just right." Long-grain or quick cooking rice would be "too soft" for the long cooking soup.

Prep: 15 minutes
Cook: 5 to 7 hours (low) or 2½ to 3½ hours (high)
Makes 6 servings

3	14-ounce cans vegetable broth
1	15-ounce can tomato puree
1	15-ounce can white or Great Northern beans, rinsed and drained
½	cup converted rice
½	cup finely chopped onion
2	cloves garlic, minced
1	teaspoon dried basil, crushed
¼	teaspoon salt
¼	teaspoon ground black pepper
8	cups coarsely chopped fresh spinach or kale leaves
	Finely shredded Parmesan cheese

1. In a 3½- or 4-quart slow cooker combine broth, tomato puree, beans, rice, onion, garlic, basil, salt, and pepper.

2. Cover; cook on low-heat setting for 5 to 7 hours or on high-heat setting for 2½ to 3½ hours.

3. Stir spinach into soup. Serve with Parmesan cheese.

Per serving: 150 cal., 3 g total fat (1 g sat. fat), 4 mg chol., 1,137 mg sodium, 31 g carb., 8 g fiber, 9 g pro.

Sloppy Vegetable Sandwiches

Instead of sandwiches, serve the vegetable mixture on tostada shells with shredded lettuce and chopped tomato for a taco-style salad.

Prep: 20 minutes
Cook: 8 to 10 hours (low) or 4 to 5 hours (high)
Makes 8 servings

1	cup chopped carrot
1	cup chopped celery
⅔	cup dry lentils, rinsed and drained
⅔	cup regular brown rice
½	cup chopped onion
1	clove garlic, minced
2	tablespoons brown sugar
2	tablespoons prepared mustard
3½	cups vegetable broth or chicken broth
1	8-ounce can tomato sauce
2	tablespoons vinegar
8	whole wheat buns or French rolls, split and toasted

1. In a 3½- or 4-quart slow cooker combine carrot, celery, dry lentils, uncooked brown rice, onion, garlic, brown sugar, and mustard. Stir in vegetable or chicken broth.

2. Cover; cook on low-heat setting for 8 to 10 hours or on high-heat setting for 4 to 5 hours.

3. Stir in tomato sauce and vinegar; cover and cook 30 minutes more.

4. To serve, spoon mixture onto toasted buns or rolls.

Per serving: 271 cal., 4 g total fat (1 g sat. fat), 0 mg chol., 864 mg sodium, 52 g carb., 0 g fiber, 11 g pro.

Ratatouille

Ratatouille

Prep: 25 minutes
Cook: 4½ to 5 hours (low) or 2 to 2½ hours (high)
Broil: 30 seconds
Makes 2 servings

1½   cups cubed, peeled (if desired) eggplant
½   cup coarsely chopped yellow summer squash or zucchini
½   cup coarsely chopped tomato
½   of an 8-ounce can no-salt-added tomato sauce
⅓   cup coarsely chopped red sweet pepper
¼   cup finely chopped onion
¼   teaspoon salt
⅛   teaspoon ground black pepper
1   clove garlic, minced
4   ½-inch-thick slices baguette-style French bread
1   teaspoon olive oil
3   tablespoons shredded Parmesan cheese
1   tablespoon snipped fresh basil

1. In a 1½-quart slow cooker, combine eggplant, squash, chopped tomato, tomato sauce, sweet pepper, onion, salt, black pepper, and garlic.

2. Cover and cook on low-heat setting for 4½ to 5 hours or on high-heat setting for 2 to 2½ hours. If no heat setting is available, cook for 4 to 4½ hours.

3. For toast: Preheat broiler. Brush one side of each bread slice with olive oil. Place slices, oiled sides up, on a baking sheet. Broil 3 to 4 inches from heat about 15 seconds or until toasted (watch carefully). Sprinkle slices with 1 tablespoon of the Parmesan cheese. Broil about 15 seconds more or until cheese melts.

4. Stir basil into mixture in cooker. Serve mixture in bowls with toast. Sprinkle with the remaining 2 tablespoons Parmesan cheese.

Per serving: 248 cal., 6 g total fat (2 g sat. fat), 5 mg chol., 739 mg sodium, 39 g carb., 6 g fiber, 10 g pro.

Creamy Tomato-Broccoli Sauce with Pasta

This no-fuss broccoli and pasta dish owes its appealing flavor to an intriguing mix of cream of mushroom soup and creamy tomato pasta sauce mix.

Prep: 15 minutes
Cook: 6 to 8 hours (low) or 3 to 4 hours (high), plus 15 minutes on high
Makes 8 to 10 servings

Nonstick cooking spray
2 14½-ounce cans diced tomatoes with basil, oregano, and garlic, undrained
2 10¾-ounce cans condensed cream of mushroom soup
1 1.3-ounce envelope creamy tomato pasta sauce mix
1 cup water
1 16-ounce package frozen cut broccoli
16 ounces dried penne or mostaccioli pasta

1. Coat a 3½- or 4-quart slow cooker with cooking spray. In a large bowl, combine undrained tomatoes, cream of mushroom soup, and dry pasta sauce mix. Stir in the water. Pour into prepared cooker.

2. Cover and cook on low-heat setting for 6 to 8 hours or on high-heat setting for 3 to 4 hours.

3. If using low-heat setting, turn to high-heat setting. Stir in broccoli; cover and cook about 15 minutes more or until broccoli is crisp-tender.

4. Meanwhile, cook pasta according to package directions; drain well. Toss pasta with sauce.
Per serving: 365 cal., 7 g total fat (2 g sat. fat), 1 mg chol., 1,270 mg sodium, 62 g carb., 4 g fiber, 12 g pro.

Sweet Beans and Lentils over Polenta

Look for refrigerated polenta in your supermarket's produce section. The varieties seasoned with wild mushrooms or Italian herbs are especially tasty in this dish.

Prep: 20 minutes
Cook: 7 to 8 hours (low) or 3½ to 4 hours (high)
Makes 6 servings

1 14-ounce can vegetable broth
1 12-ounce package frozen sweet soybeans (edamame)
1 cup dry brown lentils, rinsed and drained
1 medium red sweet pepper, chopped
½ cup water
1 teaspoon dried oregano, crushed
2 cloves garlic, minced
½ teaspoon salt
1 16-ounce tube refrigerated polenta
2 medium tomatoes, chopped

1. In a 3½- or 4-quart slow cooker, combine broth, soybeans, lentils, sweet pepper, the water, oregano, garlic, and salt.

2. Cover and cook on low-heat setting for 7 to 8 hours or on high-heat setting for 3½ to 4 hours.

3. Prepare polenta according to package directions. Stir tomatoes into lentil mixture; serve over polenta.
Per serving: 280 cal., 5 g total fat (1 g sat. fat), 0 mg chol., 794 mg sodium, 43 g carb., 15 g fiber, 19 g pro.

Pesto Beans and Pasta

Pesto Beans and Pasta

Prep: 20 minutes
Cook: 7 to 9 hours (low) or 3½ to 4½ hours (high)
Makes 6 to 8 servings

- 2   19-ounce cans cannellini beans (white kidney beans), rinsed and drained
- 1   14½-ounce can Italian-style stewed tomatoes, undrained
- 1   medium green sweet pepper, chopped
- 1   medium red sweet pepper, chopped
- 1   medium onion, cut into thin wedges
- 2   teaspoons dried Italian seasoning, crushed
- ½   teaspoon cracked black pepper
- 4   cloves garlic, minced
- ½   cup vegetable broth
- ½   cup dry white wine or canned vegetable broth
- 1   7-ounce container refrigerated basil pesto
- 12   ounces dried penne pasta
- ½   cup finely shredded Parmesan or Romano cheese

1. Combine beans, undrained tomatoes, the sweet peppers, onion, Italian seasoning, black pepper, and garlic in a 3½- or 4-quart slow cooker. Pour vegetable broth and wine over all.

2. Cover; cook on low-heat setting for 7 to 9 hours or on high-heat setting for 3½ to 4½ hours. Transfer bean mixture to a very large serving bowl using a slotted spoon, reserving cooking liquid. Stir pesto into bean mixture.

3. Meanwhile, cook pasta according to package directions; drain. Add pasta to bean mixture; gently toss to combine, adding enough of the liquid to make mixture of desired consistency. Sprinkle each serving with Parmesan cheese.

4. To serve, spoon pasta mixture into individual pasta bowls; sprinkle with additional cheese.

Per serving: 580 cal., 20 g total fat (2 g sat. fat), 10 mg chol., 843 mg sodium, 80 g carb., 11 g fiber, 25 g pro.

Mushroom Goulash

Goulash is typically a meaty dish flavored with paprika and served with noodles.

Prep: 25 minutes
Cook: 8 to 9 hours (low) or 4 to 4½ hours (high)
Makes 6 servings

- 16   ounces fresh baby portobello mushrooms, sliced
- 1   tablespoon dried minced onion
- 3   cloves garlic, minced
- 1   14-ounce can vegetable broth
- 1   14½-ounce can no-salt added diced tomatoes, undrained
- 1   6-ounce can no-salt added tomato paste
- 2   tablespoons paprika
- 1   teaspoon dried oregano, crushed
- 1   teaspoon caraway seeds
- ¼   teaspoon salt
- ¼   teaspoon ground black pepper
- ½   cup light dairy sour cream
- 8   ounces dried egg noodles, cooked and drained

1. In a 3½- to 4-quart slow cooker combine mushrooms, onion, and garlic. Stir in broth, undrained tomatoes, tomato paste, paprika, oregano, caraway seeds, salt, and pepper.

2. Cover and cook on low-heat setting for 8 to 9 hours or on high-heat setting for 4 to 4½ hours.

3. Stir sour cream into mushroom mixture before serving. Serve with hot noodles.

Per serving: 251 cal., 5 g total fat (2 g sat. fat), 43 mg chol., 443 mg sodium, 43 g carb., 5 g fiber, 12 g pro.

Lentil and Bulgur Pilaf with Feta

Five bold seasonings—garlic, oregano, cumin, coriander, and black pepper—turn vegetables, lentils, and bulgur into an extraordinary meal.

Prep: 20 minutes
Cook: 3 hours (high)
Stand: 10 minutes
Makes 6 servings

2 **14-ounce cans vegetable broth or chicken broth**
4 **medium carrots, sliced**
2 **cups loose-pack frozen whole kernel corn**
1 **cup bulgur**
½ **cup dry brown lentils, rinsed and drained**
1 **teaspoon dried oregano, crushed**
1 **teaspoon ground cumin**
¼ **teaspoon ground coriander**
¼ **teaspoon ground black pepper**
4 **cloves garlic, minced**
2 **cups chopped tomatoes**
¾ **cup crumbled feta cheese (3 ounces)**

1. In a 3½- or 4-quart slow cooker, combine broth, carrots, frozen corn, uncooked bulgur, lentils, oregano, cumin, coriander, pepper, and garlic. Cover and cook on high-heat setting for 3 hours.

2. Stir in tomatoes. Turn off cooker. Cover and let stand for 10 minutes. Sprinkle individual servings with feta cheese.

Per serving: 272 cal., 6 g total fat (3 g sat. fat), 16 mg chol., 822 mg sodium, 47 g carb., 12 g fiber, 14 g pro.

Vegetable Curry

Vary the flavor of this dish by the type of curry powder you use. Because curry powder is a mix of 16 to 20 spices, each brand is different. Try a few kinds to find the one you like best.

Prep: 25 minutes
Cook: 7 to 9 hours (low) or 3½ to 4½ hours (high)
Stand: 5 minutes
Makes 4 servings

4 **medium carrots, sliced**
2 **medium potatoes, cut into ½-inch cubes**
1 **15-ounce can garbanzo beans (chickpeas), rinsed and drained**
8 **ounces fresh green beans, cut into 1-inch pieces**
1 **cup coarsely chopped onion**
3 **cloves garlic, minced**
2 **tablespoons quick-cooking tapioca**
2 **teaspoons curry powder**
1 **teaspoon ground coriander**
¼ **to ½ teaspoon crushed red pepper**
¼ **teaspoon salt**
⅛ **teaspoon ground cinnamon**
1 **14-ounce can vegetable broth or chicken broth**
1 **14½-ounce can diced tomatoes, undrained**
   Hot cooked rice

1. In a 3½- to 5-quart slow cooker, combine carrots, potatoes, garbanzo beans, green beans, onion, garlic, tapioca, curry powder, coriander, crushed red pepper, salt, and cinnamon. Pour broth over all.

2. Cover and cook on low-heat setting for 7 to 9 hours or on high-heat setting for 3½ to 4½ hours.

3. Stir in undrained tomatoes. Cover; let stand for 5 minutes. Serve over hot cooked rice.

Per serving: 407 cal., 3 g total fat (0 g sat. fat), 0 mg chol., 1,068 mg sodium, 87 g carb., 12 g fiber, 13 g pro.

Vegetable Curry

Taste a spoonful of this **colorful curry** and you'll discover an **exquisite** combination of **spices**—curry powder, coriander, crushed red pepper, and **cinnamon.**

Smashed Potato Soup

Noodle Casserole

Tofu provides the protein for this one-dish meal.
It's a great way to add soy to your diet.

Prep: 25 minutes
Cook: 7 to 8 hours (low) or 3½ to 4 hours (high),
plus 20 minutes on high
Makes 6 servings

2½	cups water
1	10¾-ounce can reduced-fat and reduced-sodium condensed cream of mushroom soup
1	14½-ounce can no-salt-added diced tomatoes, undrained
1	cup sliced celery
1	cup sliced carrot
1	cup chopped onion
2	cloves garlic, minced
1½	teaspoons dried Italian seasoning, crushed
¼	teaspoon salt
¼	teaspoon ground black pepper
8	ounces dried extra-wide noodles
1	16-ounce package extra-firm tofu (fresh bean curd), drained if necessary, cubed
½	cup shredded reduced-fat cheddar cheese (2 ounces)

1. In a 3½- or 4-quart slow cooker, whisk together the water and cream of mushroom soup. Stir in undrained tomatoes, celery, carrot, onion, garlic, Italian seasoning, salt, and pepper.

2. Cover and cook on low-heat setting for 7 to 8 hours or high-heat setting for 3½ to 4 hours.

3. If using low-heat setting, turn to high-heat setting. Stir in uncooked noodles; cover and cook for 20 to 30 minutes more or until tender, stirring once halfway through cooking. Gently stir in tofu cubes. Sprinkle with cheese; cover and let stand until cheese is melted.

Per serving: 316 cal., 8 g total fat (2 g sat. fat), 44 mg chol., 447 mg sodium, 42 g carb., 4 g fiber, 17 g pro.

Smashed Potato Soup

Potatoes blend with cheddar cheese, cream, and roasted garlic in this chunky good-to-the-last-spoonful soup.

Prep: 25 minutes
Cook: 8 to 10 hours (low) or 4 to 5 hours (high)
Makes 8 servings

3½	pounds potatoes, cut into ¾-inch cubes
½	cup chopped yellow and/or red sweet pepper
1½	teaspoons bottled roasted garlic
½	teaspoon ground black pepper
4½	cups chicken broth
½	cup whipping cream, half-and-half, or light cream
1	cup shredded cheddar cheese (4 ounces)
½	cup thinly sliced green onions
	Sliced green onions (optional)

1. In a 4- to 6-quart slow cooker, combine potatoes, sweet pepper, garlic, and black pepper. Pour broth over all.

2. Cover and cook on low-heat setting for 8 to 10 hours or on high-heat setting for 4 to 5 hours.

3. Mash potatoes slightly with a potato masher. Stir in whipping cream, cheddar cheese, and the ½ cup thinly sliced green onions. If desired, top individual servings with additional sliced green onions.

Per serving: 243 cal., 11 g total fat (6 g sat. fat), 37 mg chol., 644 mg sodium, 30 g carb., 3 g fiber, 8 g pro.

Ravioli with Mushroom-Wine Sauce

Elegant and superbly flavored, this dish will impress company. Round out the menu with asparagus or sugar snap peas, a tossed salad, and French bread.

Prep: 20 minutes
Cook: 4 to 6 hours (low) or 2 to 3 hours (high), plus 20 minutes on high
Makes 4 main-dish servings

4	cups sliced fresh button mushrooms
4	cups sliced fresh portobello, shiitake, and/or crimini mushrooms
2	14½-ounce cans diced tomatoes, undrained
½	cup water
⅓	cup dry red wine
4	cloves garlic, minced
½	teaspoon salt
¼	teaspoon dried rosemary, crushed
¼	teaspoon crushed red pepper
1	9-ounce package refrigerated cheese-filled ravioli
	Shredded Parmesan cheese

1. In a 4- to 5-quart slow cooker combine mushrooms, undrained tomatoes, water, red wine, garlic, salt, rosemary, and crushed red pepper.

2. Cover; cook on low-heat setting for 4 to 6 hours or on high-heat setting for 2 to 3 hours.

3. If using low-heat setting, turn slow cooker to high-heat setting. Stir ravioli into soup. Cover; cook for 20 minutes more. Serve with Parmesan cheese.

Per serving: 360 cal., 7 g total fat (3 g sat. fat), 32 mg chol., 1,068 mg sodium, 62 g carb., 9 g fiber, 18 g pro.

Meatless Shepherd's Pie

The mix of white kidney beans and soybeans provides lots of protein for this potato-topped one-dish meal.

Prep: 25 minutes
Cook: 10 to 12 hours (low) or 5 to 6 hours (high), plus 30 minutes on high
Makes 8 servings

2	19-ounce cans white kidney beans (cannellini beans), rinsed and drained
1	12-ounce package frozen green soybeans (edamame)
3	carrots, peeled and sliced
1	large onion, cut into wedges
1	14½-ounce can diced tomatoes, drained
1	12-ounce jar mushroom gravy
2	cloves garlic, minced
1	24-ounce package refrigerated mashed potatoes
1	cup shredded cheddar cheese (4 ounces)

1. In a 5- to 6-quart slow cooker stir together kidney beans, soybeans, carrots, onion, tomatoes, gravy, and garlic.

2. Cover and cook on low-heat setting for 10 to 12 hours or on high-heat setting for 5 to 6 hours.

3. If using low-heat setting, turn to high-heat setting. Spoon mashed potatoes on top of bean mixture. Sprinkle with cheese. Cover and cook about 30 minutes more or until potatoes are heated through.

Per serving: 320 cal., 9 g total fat (3 g sat. fat), 15 mg chol., 805 mg sodium, 47 g carb., 13 g fiber, 20 g pro.

Ravioli with Mushroom-Wine Sauce

Marinara Sauce with Pasta

Marinara Sauce with Pasta

This easy recipe allows you to serve delicious homemade pasta sauce with fix-and-forget convenience.

Prep: 20 minutes
Cook: 8 to 10 hours (low) or 4 to 5 hours (high)
Makes 6 servings

1	28-ounce can whole Italian-style tomatoes, undrained, cut up
2	large carrots, coarsely chopped
3	stalks celery, sliced
1	large onion, chopped
1	large green sweet pepper, chopped
1	6-ounce can tomato paste
½	cup water
3	cloves garlic, minced
2	teaspoons sugar
2	teaspoons dried Italian seasoning, crushed
1	teaspoon salt
¼	teaspoon ground black pepper
1	bay leaf
12	ounces dried spaghetti or other favorite pasta
	Shredded Parmesan cheese
	Fresh herb sprigs (optional)

1. In a 3½- or 4-quart slow cooker, combine undrained tomatoes, carrots, celery, onion, sweet pepper, tomato paste, the water, garlic, sugar, Italian seasoning, salt, black pepper, and bay leaf.

2. Cover and cook on low-heat setting for 8 to 10 hours or on high-heat setting for 4 to 5 hours.

3. Discard bay leaf. Cook pasta according to package directions; drain well. Toss sauce with hot pasta. Sprinkle mixture with Parmesan cheese. If desired, garnish with fresh herb sprigs.

Per serving: 308 cal., 1 g total fat (0 g sat. fat), 0 mg chol., 636 mg sodium, 64 g carb., 6 g fiber, 11 g pro.

Mexican Minestrone

Mexican-style tomatoes and black beans turn an Italian classic into a south-of-the-border sensation.

Prep: 15 minutes
Cook: 7 to 9 hours (high)
Makes 6 to 8 servings

2   **15-ounce cans black beans, rinsed and drained**
2   **14½-ounce cans Mexican-style stewed tomatoes, undrained**
1   **15¼-ounce can whole kernel corn, rinsed and drained**
1   **14-ounce can reduced-sodium chicken broth**
2   **medium potatoes, coarsely chopped (2 cups)**
1   **cup purchased salsa**
1   **cup loose-pack frozen cut green beans**
    Dairy sour cream (optional)

1. In a 3½- or 4-quart slow cooker, combine black beans, undrained tomatoes, corn, broth, potatoes, salsa, and green beans.

2. Cover and cook on high-heat setting for 7 to 9 hours or until vegetables are tender. If desired, top individual servings with spoonfuls of sour cream.

Per serving: 250 cal., 1 g total fat (0 g sat. fat), 0 mg chol., 1,361 mg sodium, 54 g carb., 10 g fiber, 14 g pro.

Mexican Minestrone

Three-Bean Vegetarian Chili

Chocolate-flavored syrup adds an intriguing undertone to this **Cajun-accented** chili. Top each serving with a spoonful of **sour cream** and a sprinkling of **cheddar** cheese.

Three-Bean Vegetarian Chili

Prep: 20 minutes
Cook: 6 to 8 hours (low) or 3 to 4 hours (high)
Makes 4 servings

1   15-ounce can no-salt-added red kidney beans, rinsed and drained
1   15-ounce can small white beans, rinsed and drained
1   15-ounce can low-sodium black beans, rinsed and drained
1   14½-ounce can diced tomatoes and green chile peppers, undrained
1   cup beer or chicken broth
3   tablespoons chocolate-flavored syrup
1   tablespoon chili powder
2   teaspoons Cajun seasoning
    Dairy sour cream (optional)
    Shredded cheddar cheese (optional)

1. In a 3½- or 4-quart slow cooker, combine kidney beans, white beans, black beans, undrained tomatoes and green chile peppers, beer, chocolate syrup, chili powder, and Cajun seasoning.

2. Cover and cook on low-heat setting for 6 to 8 hours or on high-heat setting for 3 to 4 hours. If desired, garnish with sour cream and cheese.

Per serving: 308 cal., 1 g total fat (0 g sat. fat), 0 mg chol., 569 mg sodium, 60 g carb., 21 g fiber, 21 g pro.

White Bean and Toasted Cumin Chili

Toasting the cumin seeds intensifies their flavor, which gives the chili a rich, nutty taste.
Prep: 20 minutes
Cook: 9 to 10 hours (low) or 4½ to 5 hours (high)
Makes 4 servings

2   14½-ounce cans tomatoes, undrained, cut up
1   12-ounce can beer or nonalcoholic beer
1   cup chopped onion
3   cloves garlic, minced
1   canned chipotle chile pepper in adobo sauce, chopped (see tip, page 77)
1   tablespoon cumin seeds, toasted* and crushed
1   teaspoon sugar
½   teaspoon salt
2   19-ounce cans white kidney beans (cannellini beans), rinsed and drained
1½ cups coarsely chopped, seeded, and peeled Golden Nugget or acorn squash (about 12 ounces)
½   cup dairy sour cream
2   tablespoons lime juice
1   tablespoon snipped fresh chives
    Lime wedges (optional)

1. In a 3½- or 4-quart slow cooker, combine undrained tomatoes, beer, onion, garlic, chile pepper, cumin seeds, sugar, and salt. Stir in beans and squash.

2. Cover and cook on low-heat setting for 9 to 10 hours or on high-heat setting for 4½ to 5 hours.

3. In a small bowl, combine sour cream, lime juice, and chives. Top individual servings with sour cream mixture. If desired, garnish with lime wedges.

Per serving: 327 cal., 7 g total fat (3 g sat. fat), 11 mg chol., 1,070 mg sodium, 60 g carb., 16 g fiber, 20 g pro.

*Note: To toast cumin seeds, place the seeds in a dry skillet over low heat. Cook about 8 minutes or until fragrant, stirring often. Remove from heat; cool.

Southwestern Bean Soup

To make sure the dumplings cook through, don't lift the slow-cooker lid until you're ready to test for doneness.

Prep: 25 minutes
Cook: 10 to 12 hours (low), plus 30 minutes, or 5 to 6 hours (high), plus 20 minutes
Makes 6 servings

- 3 **cups water**
- 1 **15-ounce can red kidney beans, rinsed and drained**
- 1 **15-ounce can black beans, pinto beans, or Great Northern beans, rinsed and drained**
- 1 **14½-ounce can Mexican-style stewed tomatoes, undrained**
- 1 **10-ounce package frozen whole kernel corn**
- 1 **cup sliced carrot**
- 1 **large onion, chopped**
- 1 **4-ounce can diced green chile peppers, undrained**
- 2 **tablespoons instant beef or chicken bouillon granules**
- 1 **to 2 teaspoons chili powder**
- 2 **cloves garlic, minced**
- ⅓ **cup all-purpose flour**
- ¼ **cup yellow cornmeal**
- 1 **teaspoon baking powder**
  Dash ground black pepper
- 1 **egg white**
- 2 **tablespoons milk**
- 1 **tablespoon cooking oil**

1. In a 3½- or 4-quart slow cooker, combine the water, kidney beans, black beans, undrained tomatoes, corn, carrot, onion, undrained chile peppers, bouillon granules, chili powder, and garlic.

2. Cover and cook on low-heat setting for 10 to 12 hours or on high-heat setting for 5 to 6 hours.

3. For dumplings, in a medium bowl, stir together flour, cornmeal, baking powder, and black pepper. In a small bowl, whisk together egg white, milk, and oil. Add to flour mixture; stir with a fork just until combined.

4. Drop dumpling dough into 6 mounds on top of the bubbling soup. Cover and cook on low-heat setting about 30 minutes more or on high-heat setting about 20 minutes more or until a toothpick inserted in center of a dumpling comes out clean. (Do not lift lid while dumplings are cooking.)

Per serving: 263 cal., 4 g total fat (1 g sat. fat), 1 mg chol., 1,434 mg sodium, 51 g carb., 11 g fiber, 15 g pro.

Greek-Seasoned Lentils

Enjoy the lentils on toasted pita wedges with sliced green onions, chopped tomatoes, and sour cream.

Prep: 15 minutes
Cook: 6 to 7 hours (low) or 3 to 3½ hours (high)
Makes 6 servings

- **Nonstick cooking spray**
- 2 **cups dry brown lentils, rinsed and drained**
- 2 **cups shredded carrot**
- 1 **cup chopped onion**
- 3 **14-ounce cans vegetable broth**
- 2 **teaspoons Greek seasoning**

1. Lightly coat a 3½- to 5-quart slow cooker with cooking spray. In the prepared cooker, combine lentils, carrot, onion, broth, and Greek seasoning.

2. Cover and cook on low-heat setting for 6 to 7 hours or on high-heat setting for 3 to 3½ hours. Serve lentils with a slotted spoon.

Per serving: 260 cal., 2 g total fat (0 g sat. fat), 0 mg chol., 874 mg sodium, 45 g carb., 21 g fiber, 20 g pro.

Cajun-Seasoned Vegetarian Gumbo

With its people-pleasing mélange of Cajun seasoning, black beans, sweet peppers, and okra, this zesty gumbo will be a winner at your table.

Prep: 10 minutes
Cook: 6 to 8 hours (low) or 3 to 4 hours (high)
Makes 6 servings

2	15-ounce cans black beans, rinsed and drained
1	28-ounce can diced tomatoes, undrained
1	16-ounce package frozen (yellow, green, and red) sweet peppers and onion stir-fry vegetables
2	cups loose-pack frozen cut okra
2	to 3 teaspoons Cajun seasoning
	Hot cooked white or brown rice (optional)

1. In a 3½- or 4½-quart slow cooker, combine beans, undrained tomatoes, frozen stir-fry vegetables, frozen okra, and Cajun seasoning.

2. Cover and cook on low-heat setting for 6 to 8 hours or on high-heat setting for 3 to 4 hours. If desired, serve over hot cooked rice.

Per serving: 153 cal., 0 g total fat (0 g sat. fat), 0 mg chol., 639 mg sodium, 31 g carb., 10 g fiber, 12 g pro.

Southwestern Bean Soup

Beef Burgundy

5-ingredient meals

These recipes provide no-fuss meals and trim the grocery budget at the same time. From soup to pot roast, you can serve delicious meals with just a few ingredients at hand.

Beef Burgundy

This stew has a deep woody taste mellowed with mushrooms and stew vegetables.
Prep: 20 minutes
Cook: 7 to 9 hours (low) or 3½ to 4½ hours (high)
Makes 6 servings

- 2 **pounds beef stew meat**
- 1 **16-ounce package frozen stew vegetables**
- 1 **10¾-ounce can condensed golden mushroom soup**
- ⅔ **cup Burgundy wine**
- 1 **tablespoon quick-cooking tapioca**

1. If necessary, cut up large pieces of meat. Lightly coat a large skillet with cooking spray; heat over medium heat. Brown meat, half at a time, in hot skillet; drain off fat. Set aside.

2. Place frozen vegetables in a 3½- or 4-quart slow cooker. Top with meat. In a medium bowl stir together soup, wine, ⅓ cup water, and tapioca. Pour over meat and vegetables in cooker.

3. Cover and cook on low-heat setting for 7 to 9 hours or on high-heat setting for 3½ to 4½ hours.
Per serving: 291 cal., 8 g total fat (3 g sat. fat), 91 mg chol., 535 mg sodium, 14 g carb., 1 g fiber, 34 g pro.

Bloody Mary Steak

Sassy and lively just like the classic cocktail, this **easy-fixing** steak is **sensational** served with torn greens and steamed yellow summer squash.

Bloody Mary Steak

Prep: 20 minutes
Cook: 8 to 9 hours (low) or 4 to 4½ hours (high)
Makes 6 servings

1   **2-pound beef round steak, cut ¾ inch thick**
¾   **cup hot-style tomato juice**
2   **cloves garlic, minced**
4   **teaspoons cornstarch**
2   **teaspoons prepared horseradish**

1. Trim fat from steak. Cut steak into 6 serving-size pieces. Lightly coat an unheated large skillet with nonstick cooking spray; preheat skillet over medium-high heat. Add steak pieces; cook until brown, turning once. Place meat in a 2½- to 3½-quart slow cooker. Add tomato juice, garlic, and ¼ cup water.

2. Cover; cook on low-heat setting for 8 to 9 hours or on high-heat setting for 4 to 4½ hours.

3. Transfer meat to a serving platter, reserving cooking juices. If desired, slice meat. Cover meat and keep warm.
4. For gravy, pour cooking juices into a glass measuring cup; skim off fat. Measure juices; add water if necessary to reach 1½ cups liquid. In a small saucepan, combine cornstarch and 2 tablespoons cold water; stir in cooking juices. Cook and stir over medium heat until thickened and bubbly. Cook and stir for 2 minutes more. Stir in horseradish. Season to taste with salt and ground black pepper.
Per serving: 196 cal., 4 g total fat (1 g sat. fat), 85 mg chol., 292 mg sodium, 3 g carb., 0 g fiber, 35 g pro.

Cola Pot Roast

Prep: 15 minutes
Cook: 7 to 8 hours (low) or 3½ to 4 hours (high)
Makes 6 servings

1   **2½- to 3-pound boneless beef chuck pot roast**
2   **16-ounce packages frozen stew vegetables**
1   **12-ounce can cola**
1   **envelope (1-ounce) onion soup mix**
2   **tablespoons quick-cooking tapioca**

1. Trim fat from meat. Lightly coat a large skillet with cooking spray; heat over medium heat. Brown roast on all sides in hot skillet.

2. Place roast in a 4½ to 5-quart slow cooker. Top with frozen vegetables. In a small bowl stir together cola, soup mix, and tapioca. Pour over meat and vegetables in cooker.

3. Cover and cook on low-heat setting for 7 to 8 hours or on high-heat setting for 3½ to 4 hours.
Per serving: 278 cal., 5 g total fat (2 g sat. fat), 75 mg chol., 582 mg sodium, 28 g carb., 2 g fiber, 29 g pro.

Thai Beef

Those who love Pad Thai's signature peanut sauce will adore this easy-to-prepare dish of tender flank steak and carrots. Serve with hot cooked rice to sop up the nutty sauce.
Prep: 15 minutes
Cook: 8 to 10 hours (low) or 4 to 5 hours (high)
Makes 6 servings

1   **1½- to 2-pound beef flank steak**
1   **16-ounce package peeled baby carrots**
1   **11½-ounce bottle Thai peanut sauce**
1   **cup unsweetened coconut milk**
¼   **cup chopped dry roasted peanuts**

1. Trim fat from steak. Cut meat into thin bite-size strips. Place meat and carrots in a 3½- or 4-quart slow cooker. Pour peanut sauce over all.

2. Cover and cook on low-heat setting for 8 to 10 hours or on high-heat setting for 4 to 5 hours. Stir in coconut milk. Sprinkle each serving with peanuts.
Per serving: 449 cal., 25 g total fat (12 g sat. fat), 46 mg chol., 814 mg sodium, 23 g carb., 6 g fiber, 31 g pro.

French Dip with Portobellos

Slices of meaty portobello mushrooms add a savory new dimension to French dip sandwiches. Pour the seasoned broth into individual bowls large enough to dunk a corner of the sandwich.

Prep: 25 minutes
Cook: 8 to 9 hours (low) or 4 to 4½ hours (high)
Stand: 10 minutes
Makes 8 sandwiches

- 1   3- to 3½-pound beef bottom round or rump roast
- 4   portobello mushrooms (3 to 4 inches in diameter)
- 1   14½-ounce can beef broth seasoned with onion
- 8   hoagie buns, split and toasted

1. Trim fat from roast. If necessary, cut roast to fit into a 3½- to 6-quart slow cooker. In a large skillet brown meat on all sides in hot oil. Drain off fat. Transfer meat to cooker.

2. Clean mushrooms; remove and discard stems. Cut mushrooms into ¼-inch slices. Add to cooker. Pour broth over meat and mushrooms.

3. Cover and cook on low-heat setting for 8 to 9 hours or on high-heat setting for 4 to 4½ hours. Remove meat from cooker; cover and let stand for 10 minutes.

4. Meanwhile, using a slotted spoon, remove mushrooms and set aside. Thinly slice meat. Arrange meat and mushroom slices on toasted buns. Pour cooking juices into a measuring cup; skim off fat. Drizzle a little of the juices onto each sandwich and pour the remaining juices into individual bowls; serve with sandwiches for dipping.

Per serving: 780 cal., 33 g total fat (11 g sat. fat), 106 mg chol., 955 mg sodium, 73 g carb., 4 g fiber, 47 g pro.

Easy Cheesy Sloppy Joes

This is a kid favorite that adults like too. Sweet pickle slices taste great on top of the meat.

Prep: 20 minutes
Cook: 4½ to 5 hours (low) or 2 to 2½ hours (high)
Makes 16 servings

- 2½   pounds lean ground beef
- 1   cup chopped onion
- 2   10¾-ounce cans condensed fiesta nacho cheese soup
- ¾   cup ketchup
- 16   hamburger buns, split and toasted

1. In a 12-inch skillet cook ground beef and onion over medium heat until meat is brown and onion is tender. Drain off fat.

2. In a 3½- or 4-quart slow cooker combine meat mixture, soup, and ketchup.

3. Cover and cook on low-heat setting for 4½ to 5 hours or on high-heat setting for 2 to 2½ hours. Serve meat mixture in toasted buns.

Per serving: 389 cal., 22 g total fat (9 g sat. fat), 63 mg chol., 680 mg sodium, 29 g carb., 2 g fiber, 17 g pro.

French Dip with Portobellos

Meatball and Vegetable Stew

Keep the ingredients for this **hearty stew** on hand in the **pantry** so you can prepare it **easily** at the start of a **busy day**.

Meatball and Vegetable Stew

Prep: 10 minutes
Cook: 6 to 8 hours (low) or 3 to 4 hours (high)
Makes 4 servings

1	16- to 18-ounce package frozen cooked meatballs
½	of a 16-ounce package (about 2 cups) frozen mixed vegetables
1	14½-ounce can diced tomatoes with onion and garlic, or stewed tomatoes, undrained
1	12-ounce jar mushroom gravy
1½	teaspoons dried basil, crushed

1. In a 3½- or 4-quart slow cooker place meatballs and mixed vegetables. In a bowl stir together tomatoes, gravy, basil, and ⅓ cup water; pour over meatballs and vegetables.

2. Cover and cook on low-heat setting for 6 to 8 hours or on high-heat setting for 3 to 4 hours.

Per serving: 472 cal., 32 g total fat (14 g sat. fat), 87 mg chol., 1,883 mg sodium, 26 g carb., 6 g fiber, 21 g pro.

Taco Chili

Prep: 10 minutes
Cook: 4 to 6 hours (low) or 2 to 3 hours (high)
Makes 4 to 6 servings

1	pound ground beef
1	1.2-ounce package taco seasoning mix
2	15-ounce cans chunky Mexican-style tomatoes, undrained
1	15-ounce can red kidney beans, undrained
1	15-ounce can whole kernel corn, undrained

1. In a large skillet cook ground beef until browned, drain.

2. In a 3½- to 4-quart slow cooker combine the cooked ground beef, taco seasoning mix, undrained tomatoes, undrained beans, and undrained corn. Cover and cook on low-heat setting for 4 to 6 hours or on high-heat setting for 2 to 3 hours.

Per serving: 464 cal., 17 g total fat (6 g sat. fat), 71 mg chol., 2,317 mg sodium, 50 g carb., 9 g fiber, 33 g pro.

Mexican Lasagna

The layers are tender, the flavor is full and zesty. Best of all, there's no scooping necessary— after standing, this lasagna holds a soft-cut edge.
Prep: 25 minutes
Cook: 3 to 4 hours (low)
Stand: 15 minutes
Makes 8 servings

1½	pounds bulk pork sausage
9	6-inch corn tortillas
1	11-ounce can whole kernel corn with sweet peppers, drained
2	cups shredded taco cheese (8 ounces)
1	19-ounce can enchilada sauce

1. Lightly coat a 3½- or 4-quart slow cooker with cooking spray; set aside. In a large skillet cook sausage until brown; drain off fat.

2. Place 3 of the tortillas in the bottom of the prepared cooker, overlapping as necessary. Top with half of the sausage and half of the corn. Sprinkle with ½ cup of the cheese. Pour about ¾ cup of the enchilada sauce over layers in cooker. Repeat with 3 more tortillas, remaining sausage, and remaining corn. Sprinkle with ½ cup of the cheese. Pour ¾ cup enchilada sauce over cheese. Top with remaining 3 tortillas, remaining 1 cup cheese, and remaining enchilada sauce.

3. Cover and cook on low-heat setting for 3 to 4 hours. Remove liner from cooker, if possible, or turn off cooker. Let stand, covered, 15 minutes before serving.

Per serving: 512 cal., 34 g total fat (15 g sat. fat), 71 mg chol., 1,082 mg sodium, 27 g carb., 3 g fiber, 18 g pro.

Pork Chops and Corn Bread Stuffing

Prep: 20 minutes
Cook: 5 to 6 hours (low) or 2½ to 3 hours (high)
Makes 4 servings

4   pork rib chops, cut ¾-inch thick
1   10¾-ounce can condensed golden
    mushroom or cream of mushroom soup
¼   cup butter or margarine, melted
1   16-ounce package frozen loose-pack
    broccoli, cauliflower, and carrots
½   of a 16-ounce package corn bread stuffing
    mix (about 3 cups)

1. Lightly coat a 5½- or 6-quart slow cooker with cooking spray; set aside. Lightly coat a 10-inch skillet with cooking spray; heat over medium heat. Brown the chops, half at a time, in the hot skillet. Remove chops from skillet and set aside.

2. In a very large bowl stir together the soup and melted butter. Add frozen vegetables and stuffing mix; stir to combine. Transfer mixture to prepared cooker. Arrange chops on top of stuffing mixture.

3. Cover and cook on low-heat setting for 5 to 6 hours or on high-heat setting for 2½ to 3 hours.

Per serving: 558 cal., 22 g total fat (10 g sat. fat), 89 mg chol., 1,533 mg sodium, 56 g carb., 7 g fiber, 30 g pro.

Cajun Pork

Prep: 20 minutes
Cook: 6 to 7 hours (low) or 3 to 3½ hours (high), plus 30 minutes on high
Makes 6 to 8 servings

2½ to 3 pounds boneless pork shoulder,
    trimmed and cut into 1-inch cubes
2   medium yellow sweet peppers, cut into
    1-inch pieces
1   tablespoon Cajun seasoning

1   14½-ounce can diced tomatoes with green
    pepper and onion, undrained
1   16-ounce package frozen cut okra
    Bottled hot pepper sauce (optional)

1. Lightly coat a large skillet with cooking spray. Heat over medium heat. In hot skillet cook meat, half at a time, until brown; drain off fat.

2. In a 3½- or 4-quart slow cooker place meat and sweet peppers. Sprinkle with Cajun seasoning. Top with undrained tomatoes.

3. Cover and cook on low-heat setting for 6 to 7 hours or on high-heat setting for 3 to 3½ hours.

4. If using low-heat setting, turn to high-heat setting. Stir in frozen okra. Cover and cook 30 minutes more. If desired, pass hot pepper sauce.

Per serving: 233 cal., 8 g total fat (3 g sat. fat), 77 mg chol., 444 mg sodium, 15 g carb., 4 g fiber, 25 g pro.

Spicy Ham and Garbanzo Bean Soup

Prep: 15 minutes
Cook: 7 to 9 hours (low) or 3½ to 4½ hours (high)
Makes 6 servings

1½ cups cubed cooked ham (8 ounces)
1   15-ounce can garbanzo beans (chickpeas),
    rinsed and drained
2   cups sliced carrots
1   cup sliced celery
4   cups hot-style vegetable juice

1. In a 3½- or 4½-quart slow cooker combine ham, beans, carrots, and celery. Pour vegetable juice and 1 cup water over all.

2. Cover and cook on low-heat setting for 7 to 9 hours or on high-heat setting for 3½ to 4½ hours.

Per serving: 187 cal., 5 g total fat (1 g sat. fat), 22 mg chol., 1,272 mg sodium, 23 g carb., 5 g fiber, 12 g pro.

Pork Chops and Corn Bread Stuffing

Cranberry Chicken

Cranberry Chicken

Rice and steamed Brussels sprouts make eye-catching, taste-tempting partners for this savory fruited chicken. For a change of pace, prepare your favorite recipe for rice pilaf and substitute it for the plain hot cooked rice.

Prep: 15 minutes
Cook: 5 to 6 hours (low) or 2½ to 3 hours (high)
Makes 6 servings

2½	to 3 pounds chicken thighs and/or drumsticks, skinned
1	16-ounce can whole cranberry sauce
2	tablespoons dry onion soup mix
2	tablespoons quick-cooking tapioca
3	cups hot cooked rice

1. Place chicken pieces in a 3½- or 4-quart slow cooker. In a small bowl, stir together cranberry sauce, dry soup mix, and tapioca. Pour over chicken pieces.

2. Cover; cook on low-heat setting for 5 to 6 hours or on high-heat setting for 2½ to 3 hours. Serve chicken and sauce over hot cooked rice.

Per serving: 357 cal., 4 g total fat (1 g sat. fat), 89 mg chol., 268 mg sodium, 55 g carb., 1 g fiber, 23 g pro.

Chicken with Sweet Potatoes

Feel like something sweet tonight? Indulge yourself with a medley of honey, savory onions, and vitamin-rich sweet potatoes.

Prep: 20 minutes
Cook: 7 to 9 hours (low) or 3½ to 4½ hours (high)
Makes 6 servings

6	medium sweet potatoes, peeled and quartered (about 2½ pounds)
1	small onion, cut into thin wedges
2	to 2½ pounds chicken thighs and/or drumsticks, skinned
¾	cup bottled honey-mustard salad dressing
½	teaspoon dried rosemary, crushed

1. In a 4½- to 6-quart slow cooker place sweet potatoes and onion wedges. Place chicken pieces over vegetables.

2. In a small bowl stir together salad dressing and rosemary. Pour dressing over chicken.

3. Cover and cook on low-heat setting for 7 to 9 hours or on high-heat setting for 3½ to 4½ hours. Using a slotted spoon, transfer chicken and vegetables to a serving platter. Whisk cooking liquid until smooth; serve with chicken and vegetables.

Per serving: 378 cal., 16 g total fat (2 g sat. fat), 71 mg chol., 186 mg sodium, 40 g carb., 4 g fiber, 19 g pro.

Finger Lickin' Barbecue Chicken

This recipe's secrets come from unexpected sources: the hot dog stand (mustard) and the breakfast table (preserves).

Prep: 10 minutes
Cook: 6 to 8 hours (low) or 3 to 4 hours (high)
Makes 4 to 6 servings

2½	to 3 pounds chicken drumsticks, skinned (if desired)
1	cup bottled barbecue sauce
⅓	cup apricot or peach preserves
2	teaspoons yellow mustard

1. Place chicken in a 3½- or 4-quart slow cooker. In a small bowl stir together the barbecue sauce, preserves, and mustard. Pour over chicken.

2. Cover and cook on low-heat setting for 6 to 8 hours or on high-heat setting for 3 to 4 hours. Remove chicken to serving dish; cover and keep warm. If desired, transfer sauce mixture in cooker to a medium saucepan. Bring to boiling; reduce heat. Simmer, uncovered, for 10 minutes or until desired consistency. Serve sauce with chicken.

Per serving: 456 cal., 17 g total fat (4 g sat. fat), 154 mg chol., 963 mg sodium, 37 g carb., 2 g fiber, 38 g pro.

Pesto-Sauce Chicken

A bed of colorful pasta makes the ideal backdrop for showing off this luscious creamy chicken and vegetable entrée. If you like, garnish each serving with a sprig of basil.

Prep: 20 minutes
Cook: 5 to 6 hours (low) or 2½ to 3 hours (high)
Makes 6 servings

   2   pounds skinless, boneless chicken thighs, cut into 1-inch pieces
 1½   cups purchased Alfredo pasta sauce
   ¼   cup purchased basil pesto
   1   16-ounce package loose-pack frozen stir-fry onion and sweet pepper mix
   3   cups hot cooked spinach linguine

1. Coat an unheated large nonstick skillet with cooking spray. Preheat over medium heat. Add chicken, half at a time; cook until brown. In a 3½- or 4-quart slow cooker, combine chicken, Alfredo sauce, and pesto. Stir in frozen vegetables.

2. Cover; cook on low-heat setting for 5 to 6 hours or on high-heat setting for 2½ to 3 hours. Serve over hot cooked linguine.

Per serving: 470 cal., 20 g total fat (6 g sat. fat), 160 mg chol., 600 mg sodium, 27 g carb., 2 g fiber, 43 g pro.

Red Beans over Spanish Rice

Tender red beans go from tame to sassy when mixed with cumin. Slice lime wedges to serve on the side: A spritz of citrus is a nice twist.

Prep: 25 minutes
Cook: 10 to 11 hours (low) or 5 to 5½ hours (high)
Stand: 1 hour
Makes 6 to 8 servings

   2   cups dry red beans or dry red kidney beans
 2½   cups chopped onion
   1   tablespoon bottled minced garlic (6 cloves)
   1   tablespoon ground cumin
   1   6¾-ounce package Spanish rice mix
        Lime wedges (optional)

1. Rinse beans. In a large saucepan combine dry beans and 5 cups water. Bring to boiling; reduce heat. Simmer, uncovered, for 10 minutes. Remove from heat. Cover and let stand for 1 hour. (Or place beans in 5 cups of water in saucepan. Cover and let soak in a cool place for 6 to 8 hours or overnight.) Drain and rinse beans.

2. Lightly coat the inside of a 3½- or 4-quart slow cooker with nonstick cooking spray. In the prepared cooker place beans, 4 cups water, onion, garlic, and cumin.

3. Cover and cook on low-heat setting for 10 to 11 hours or on high-heat setting for 5 to 5½ hours. Prepare the rice mix according to package directions. Remove beans from cooker using a slotted spoon. Serve beans over cooked rice. If desired, spoon some of the cooking liquid from the cooker over each serving and squeeze lime juice over beans and rice.

Per serving: 344 cal., 1 g total fat (0 g sat. fat), 0 mg chol., 450 mg sodium, 68 g carb., 17 g fiber, 19 g pro.

Pesto-Sauce Chicken

Spinach pasta adds a **rich color** to this creamy chicken and vegetable dish. If you like, add a sprig of basil for a **finishing touch**.

quick **dinner breads**

Bread and a dish from your slow cooker is often all you need for a complete meal. With these quick-to-fix ideas, you can have fresh homemade bread in a flash.

Focaccia Breadsticks
Makes 16 breadsticks

Preheat oven to 350°F. Drain
1/4 cup oil-packed dried tomatoes,
reserving oil; finely snip tomatoes.
In a large bowl, combine tomatoes,
2 teaspoons of the reserved oil,
1/4 cup grated Romano cheese,
2 teaspoons water, and
1/8 teaspoon cracked black pepper.

   Unroll one 13.8-ounce package
refrigerated pizza dough. On a
lightly floured surface, roll the
dough into a 14×8-inch rectangle.
Spread the tomato mixture
crosswise over half of the dough.
Fold plain dough half over filled
dough half to make a 7×8-inch
rectangle; press lightly to seal
edges. Cut the rectangle crosswise
into sixteen 1/2-inch-wide strips.
Twist each strip two or three
times. Place strips 1 inch apart
on a lightly greased baking sheet.
Bake for 15 to 18 minutes or until
golden. Cool on a wire rack. Serve
warm or at room temperature.
Per serving: 72 cal., 1 g total fat
(0 g sat. fat), 1 mg chol., 159 mg sodium, 12 g carb.,
0 g fiber, 3 g pro.

Herbed Crouton Sticks
Makes 12 to 16 sticks

Preheat oven to 400°F. Cut an
8-ounce baguette-style French
bread loaf in half horizontally. Cut
bread into 1-inch-wide sticks that
are 4 to 6 inches long (you should
have 12 to 16 sticks). Place
breadsticks in a shallow baking
pan. In a small bowl, mix 1/4 cup
butter, melted; 1 tablespoon
snipped fresh basil or 1/2 teaspoon
dried basil, crushed; and
1/4 teaspoon garlic salt. Brush
breadsticks on all sides with butter
mixture. Bake for 12 to 15 minutes
or until golden, turning once.
Per serving: 86 cal., 4 g total fat (3 g sat. fat),
10 mg chol., 162 mg sodium, 10 g carb.,
1 g fiber, 2 g pro.

Soft Pretzels
Makes 12 pretzels

Preheat oven to 375°F. Grease a
baking sheet. Unroll one 11-ounce
package (12) refrigerated
breadsticks so breadsticks lay
flat. Gently pull each breadstick
into a 16-inch rope. Shape each
rope into a pretzel by first
crossing one end over the other
about 4 inches from each end to
form a circle. Take an end in each
hand and twist once at the
overlap point. Carefully lift each
end across to the edge of the
circle opposite to finish the
pretzel shape. Moisten the ends;
press to seal.

   Place pretzels on prepared
baking sheet. In a small bowl,
whisk together 1 egg white and
1 tablespoon water; brush over
pretzels. Sprinkle with poppy
and/or sesame seeds. Bake for
12 to 15 minutes or until golden.
Per serving: 73 cal., 1 g total fat
(0 g sat. fat), 0 mg chol., 190 mg sodium, 13 g carb.,
0 g fiber, 2 g pro.

Broccoli Corn Bread
Makes 16 servings

Preheat oven to 350°F. Grease a 9×9×2-inch baking pan; set aside. In a large bowl, beat 3 eggs with a whisk or rotary beater; stir in one 8½-ounce package corn muffin mix. Stir in 2 cups shredded cheddar cheese (8 ounces); one 10-ounce package frozen chopped broccoli, thawed (2 cups); and ½ cup chopped onion. Spoon into prepared baking pan. Bake for 25 to 30 minutes or until a toothpick inserted near the center comes out clean. Serve warm.

Per serving: 138 cal., 7 g total fat (3 g sat. fat), 55 mg chol., 211 mg sodium, 12 g carb., 1 g fiber, 6 g pro.

Simple Focaccia
Makes 12 servings

Preheat oven to 375°F. Lightly grease a 12- to 14-inch pizza pan; set aside.

Prepare one 16-ounce package hot roll mix according to package directions for basic dough, except use 1 egg and substitute 2 tablespoons olive oil for the margarine. Knead dough; allow to rest as directed. Roll dough into a 12-inch round. Place dough in prepared pan.

With your fingertips, press indentations randomly in dough. Brush dough with 1 tablespoon olive oil; sprinkle with 1 tablespoon snipped fresh rosemary and 2 tablespoons coarse salt.

Bake for 15 to 20 minutes or until golden. Cool on a wire rack for 10 minutes. Remove from pan; cool completely.

Per serving: 176 cal., 4 g total fat (1 g sat. fat), 18 mg chol., 1,191 mg sodium, 29 g carb., 0 g fiber, 6 g pro.

Cheese-Herb Biscuits
Makes 10 to 12 biscuits

Preheat oven to 450°F. In a large bowl, stir together 2 cups all-purpose flour, 4 teaspoons baking powder, and ½ teaspoon salt. Using a pastry blender, cut in ¼ cup shortening until mixture resembles coarse crumbs. Stir in ¾ cup shredded Gruyère cheese (3 ounces) and 2 tablespoons snipped fresh dill. Make a well in the center of the flour-cheese mixture. Add ⅔ cup milk all at once. Using a fork, stir just until moistened.

On a lightly floured surface, quickly knead dough for 10 to 12 strokes or until nearly smooth. Pat dough to ½-inch thickness. Cut dough with a floured 2½-inch scalloped round cutter. Place biscuits on an ungreased baking sheet. Bake for 10 to 12 minutes or until golden. Serve warm.

Per serving: 174 cal., 8 g total fat (3 g sat. fat), 10 mg chol., 311 mg sodium, 19 g carb., 1 g fiber, 5 g pro.

Cheesy Cauliflower for a Crowd

side dishes

Perfect for rounding out almost any menu, these slow-cooked vegetables, breads, and desserts are ideal for toting to potlucks and picnics or for freeing up oven or stove-top space when you need to prepare several dishes for an elaborate meal.

Cheesy Cauliflower for a Crowd

Cheddar cheese pasta sauce makes this cauliflower potluck pleaser oh-so-easy and oh-so-cheesy.

Prep: 20 minutes   **Cook:** 6 to 7 hours (low) or 3 to 3½ hours (high)
Makes 10 to 12 servings

8	**cups cauliflower florets**
1	**large onion, thinly sliced**
½	**teaspoon fennel seeds, crushed**
1	**14- to 16-ounce jar cheddar cheese pasta sauce**
	Ground black pepper (optional)

1. In a 3½- or 4-quart slow cooker, combine cauliflower, onion, and fennel seeds. Pour pasta sauce over all.

2. Cover and cook on low-heat setting for 6 to 7 hours or on high-heat setting for 3 to 3½ hours. Stir gently. If desired, sprinkle with pepper before serving.

Per serving: 59 cal., 6 g total fat (2 g sat. fat), 16 mg chol., 329 mg sodium, 8 g carb., 2 g fiber, 3 g pro.

Cues for Cleanup

Cleaning a slow cooker after a meal can be quick and easy if you remember these tips. Before you start, let the ceramic liner of your slow cooker cool to room temperature so it doesn't crack when it comes in contact with water. If the liner is removable, simply put it in the dishwasher. If it's permanently attached to the base, clean it with a soft cloth and warm soapy water. Don't use abrasive cleaners or pads because they can damage the surface. If food is stuck on, fill the liner with warm water and let it stand before cleaning it or putting it in the dishwasher. Wipe the base clean with a damp cloth.

A **tangy mustard-dill sauce** makes this crisp green beans and tender potatoes recipe the **perfect accompaniment** to Sunday dinner's roast, beef tenderloin, or salmon.

Saucy Green Beans and Potatoes

Saucy Green Beans and Potatoes

Prep: 20 minutes
Cook: 6 to 8 hours (low) or 3 to 4 hours (high)
Makes 12 servings

- 2 pounds new potatoes, halve any large ones
- 1 pound fresh green beans, trimmed and halved crosswise
- 1 10¾-ounce can condensed cream of celery soup
- ¾ cup water
- ¼ cup Dijon-style mustard
- ¾ teaspoon dried dillweed

1. Place potatoes and green beans in a 3½- or 4-quart slow cooker. Combine soup, water, mustard, and dillweed. Pour over vegetables; gently stir to combine.

2. Cover; cook on low-heat setting for 6 to 8 hours or on high-heat setting for 3 to 4 hours. Gently stir before serving.

Per serving: 95 cal., 2 g total fat (1 g sat. fat), 1 mg chol., 313 mg sodium, 17 g carb., 3 g fiber, 3 g pro.

Parmesan Cheese Bread

Slices of this spunky steamed bread are the perfect serve-along for spaghetti and meatballs or lasagna.

Prep: 15 minutes
Cook: 1¾ hours (high)
Cool: 10 minutes
Makes 12 servings

- 1¾ cups packaged biscuit mix
- ¼ cup grated Parmesan cheese (1 ounce)
- 1 teaspoon dried basil, crushed
- 2 eggs, slightly beaten
- ⅓ cup milk
- 2 tablespoons snipped oil-packed sun-dried tomatoes, well drained

1. Grease two 1-pint straight-sided, wide-mouth canning jars well; flour the greased jars. Set aside.

2. In a medium bowl combine biscuit mix, Parmesan cheese, and basil. In a small bowl combine eggs and milk; add to flour mixture and stir just until moistened. Stir in drained tomatoes.

3. Divide mixture between prepared jars. Cover jars tightly with greased foil, greased side down. Place jars in a 4- to 6-quart slow cooker. Pour ½ cup warm water into slow cooker around jars.

4. Cover and cook on high-heat setting about 1¾ hours or until a wooden skewer inserted in center of each comes out clean. Remove jars from slow cooker. Cool for 10 minutes. Remove bread from jars. Cool completely before slicing.

Per serving: 96 cal., 4 g total fat (1 g sat. fat), 37 mg chol., 260 mg sodium, 12 g carb., 0 g fiber, 3 g pro.

Caramelized Onions and Potatoes

Sweet onions are special varieties that are juicier, contain more sugar, and have a less pungent flavor than regular onions.

Prep: 15 minutes
Cook: 6 to 7 hours (low) or 3 to 3½ hours (high)
Makes 6 servings

2	large sweet onions (such as Vidalia, Maui, or Walla Walla), thinly sliced
1½	pounds tiny new potatoes, halved
¼	cup butter, melted
½	cup beef or chicken broth
3	tablespoons packed brown sugar
½	teaspoon salt
¼	teaspoon ground black pepper
	Ground black pepper (optional)

1. In a 3½- or 4-quart slow cooker, combine onions and potatoes.

2. In a small bowl, combine melted butter, broth, brown sugar, salt, and the ¼ teaspoon pepper. Pour mixture over onions and potatoes in cooker.

3. Cover and cook on low-heat setting for 6 to 7 hours or on high-heat setting for 3 to 3½ hours. Stir gently before serving. Serve with a slotted spoon. If desired, sprinkle with additional pepper.

Per serving: 194 cal., 8 g total fat (5 g sat. fat), 22 mg chol., 356 mg sodium, 28 g carb., 3 g fiber, 3 g pro.

Apple Bread

Slow cookers are made-to-order for steaming breads such as these fruit and nut loaves.

Prep: 20 minutes
Cook: 1¾ to 2 hours (high)
Cool: 10 minutes
Makes 2 loaves (6 servings per loaf)

1	cup all-purpose flour
1½	teaspoons baking powder
1	teaspoon apple pie spice
¼	teaspoon salt
½	cup packed brown sugar
2	tablespoons cooking oil or melted butter
2	eggs, lightly beaten
½	cup applesauce
½	cup chopped walnuts, toasted
½	cup warm water

1. Grease two 1-pint, straight-sided, wide-mouth canning jars well; flour the greased jars. Set aside.

2. In a medium bowl, combine flour, baking powder, apple pie spice, and salt. Make a well in the center of the flour mixture; set aside.

3. In a small bowl, combine brown sugar, oil, eggs, and applesauce. Add applesauce mixture all at once to the flour mixture. Stir just until moistened. Stir in walnuts.

4. Divide mixture between the prepared canning jars. Cover the jars tightly with greased foil, greased sides in. Place the jars in a 4- to 6-quart slow cooker. Pour the warm water into the cooker around the jars.

5. Cover and cook on high-heat setting for 1¾ to 2 hours or until a long wooden skewer inserted near the center of each comes out clean.

6. Remove jars from cooker; place on a wire rack. Cool for 10 minutes. Carefully remove bread from jars. Serve warm.

Per serving: 146 cal., 7 g total fat (1 g sat. fat), 35 mg chol., 113 mg sodium, 20 g carb., 1 g fiber, 3 g pro.

Caramelized Onions and Potatoes

Caramelized onions and a little brown sugar add just the right **hint** of sweetness to this **first-rate** potato dish. Team it with steaks, chops, or your favorite **roasted meats**.

Acorn Squash with Orange-Cranberry Sauce

Acorn Squash with Orange-Cranberry Sauce

Whether you serve this festive cranberry-sauce squash with meat, poultry, or fish, it's a delicious way to round out a meal.

Prep: 15 minutes
Cook: 6 to 7 hours (low) or 3 to 3½ hours (high)
Makes 4 to 6 servings

2	**medium acorn squash (about 2 pounds)**
1	**16-ounce can jellied cranberry sauce**
¼	**cup orange marmalade**
¼	**cup raisins**
¼	**teaspoon ground cinnamon**
	Salt
	Ground black pepper

1. Cut each squash in half lengthwise; remove and discard seeds. Cut squash into 1-inch-thick wedges. Arrange squash in a 3½- or 4-quart slow cooker.

2. In a small saucepan, combine cranberry sauce, marmalade, raisins, and cinnamon; heat and stir until smooth. Pour over squash pieces in cooker.

3. Cover and cook on low-heat setting for 6 to 7 hours or on high-heat setting for 3 to 3½ hours. Season to taste with salt and pepper.

Per serving: 328 cal., 0 g total fat (0 g sat. fat), 0 mg chol., 220 mg sodium, 83 g carb., 5 g fiber, 2 g pro.

Boston Brown Bread

Slathered with butter or cream cheese, this bread is delightful with everything from meats and soups to main-dish salads.

Prep: 20 minutes
Cook: 2 hours (high)
Cool: 10 minutes
Makes 2 loaves (6 servings per loaf)

½	cup whole wheat flour
⅓	cup all-purpose flour
¼	cup cornmeal
½	teaspoon baking powder
¼	teaspoon baking soda
⅛	teaspoon salt
1	egg
¾	cup buttermilk
¼	cup molasses
2	tablespoons packed brown sugar
1	tablespoon butter, melted
2	tablespoons raisins, finely chopped
½	cup warm water

1. Grease two 1-pint, straight-sided, wide-mouth canning jars well; set aside.

2. In a medium bowl, stir together whole wheat flour, all-purpose flour, cornmeal, baking powder, baking soda, and salt. Make a well in the center of the flour mixture; set aside.

3. In a small bowl, whisk together egg, buttermilk, molasses, brown sugar, and melted butter. Add egg mixture to flour mixture, stirring just until combined. Stir in raisins.

4. Divide mixture between the prepared canning jars; cover the jars tightly with greased foil, greased sides in. Immediately set jars in a 4- to 6-quart slow cooker. Pour the warm water into the cooker around the jars.

5. Cover and cook on high-heat setting about 2 hours or until a long wooden skewer inserted near the center of each comes out clean.

6. Remove jars from cooker; place on a wire rack. Cool for 10 minutes. Carefully remove bread from jars. Cool on wire rack. Serve bread warm or at room temperature.

Per serving: 89 cal., 2 g total fat (1 g sat. fat), 21 mg chol., 102 mg sodium, 17 g carb., 1 g fiber, 2 g pro.

Hash Browns with Garlic-Mushroom Sauce

Prep: 15 minutes
Cook: 8 to 9 hours (low) or 4 to 4 ½ hours (high)
Makes 8 to 10 servings

1	32-ounce package frozen loose-pack diced hash brown potatoes
2	cups shredded Swiss cheese (8 ounces)
2	4-ounce cans (drained weight) sliced mushrooms, drained
1	tablespoon bottled roasted minced garlic
1	10¾-ounce can condensed cream of mushroom soup
¼	cup water

1. In a 3½- or 4-quart slow cooker, combine frozen potatoes, cheese, drained mushrooms, and garlic. Add cream of mushroom soup and the water; stir to combine.

2. Cover and cook on low-heat setting for 8 to 9 hours or on high-heat setting for 4 to 4½ hours. Stir gently before serving.

Per serving: 248 cal., 11 g total fat (6 g sat. fat), 26 mg chol., 482 mg sodium, 26 g carb., 3 g fiber, 12 g pro.

Savory Stuffing with Fruit and Pecans

Cooking the stuffing in the slow cooker leaves space in the oven for other dishes.

Prep: 25 minutes
Cook: 4½ to 5 hours (low) or 2¼ to 2½ hours (high)
Makes 10 to 12 servings

½	cup apple juice
1½	cups package mixed dried fruit bits (6-ounce)
½	cup butter or margarine
1	cup finely chopped celery
½	cup sliced green onions
2	tablespoons snipped fresh parsley
1	teaspoon dried sage, crushed
½	teaspoon dried thyme, crushed
½	teaspoon dried marjoram, crushed
½	teaspoon salt
¼	teaspoon ground black pepper
10	cups dry bread cubes*
½	cup broken pecans, toasted
1	to 1½ cups chicken broth

1. In a small saucepan, heat apple juice until boiling. Stir in dried fruit. Remove from heat. Cover; let stand.

2. Meanwhile, in a medium saucepan, melt butter over medium heat. Add celery and green onions; cook until tender. Remove from heat. Stir in parsley, sage, thyme, marjoram, salt, and pepper.

3. Place dry bread cubes in a large bowl. Add undrained fruit, vegetable mixture, and pecans. Drizzle with enough of the broth to moisten, tossing lightly. Transfer to a 3½- or 4-quart slow cooker.

4. Cover and cook on low-heat setting for 4½ to 5 hours or on high-heat setting for 2¼ to 2½ hours.

Per serving: 279 cal., 15 g total fat (7 g sat. fat), 27 mg chol., 528 mg sodium, 33 g carb., 2 g fiber, 4 g pro.

*Note: To prepare the 10 cups dry bread cubes, preheat oven to 300°F. Cut 14 to 16 slices of bread into ½-inch cubes; spread in a large roasting pan. Bake for 10 to 15 minutes or until dry, stirring twice.

Creamy Potato Wedges

Sour cream dip, two cheeses, and mayonnaise turn refrigerated potato wedges into a company-special dish.

Prep: 10 minutes
Cook: 3½ to 4½ hours (low) or 1¾ to 2¼ hours (high)
Makes 8 servings

2	8-ounce containers dairy sour cream chive dip
1	cup finely shredded Asiago cheese (4 ounces)
1	3-ounce package cream cheese, cut up
½	cup mayonnaise
2	20-ounce packages refrigerated new potato wedges
	Snipped fresh chives (optional)

1. In a 3½- or 4-quart slow cooker, combine sour cream dip, Asiago cheese, cream cheese, and mayonnaise. Stir in potatoes.

2. Cover and cook on low-heat setting for 3½ to 4½ hours or on high-heat setting for 1¾ to 2¼ hours. Stir gently before serving. If desired, sprinkle with fresh chives.

Per serving: 415 cal., 31 g total fat (14 g sat. fat), 55 mg chol., 835 mg sodium, 23 g carb., 4 g fiber, 10 g pro.

Creamy Potato Wedges

Creamy Wild Rice Pilaf

Creamy Wild Rice Pilaf

Paired with roasted chicken or broiled salmon and steamed broccoli, this earthy jeweled pilaf is an easy side dish for a colorful meal.

Prep: 20 minutes
Cook: 7 to 8 hours (low) or 3½ to 4 hours (high)
Makes 12 servings

- 1 cup wild rice, rinsed and drained
- 1 cup regular brown rice
- 1 10¾-ounce can condensed cream of mushroom with roasted garlic or condensed golden mushroom soup
- 1 cup sliced fresh mushrooms
- 1 cup shredded carrots
- ½ cup sliced celery
- ⅓ cup chopped onion
- ¼ cup snipped dried apricots
- 1 teaspoon dried thyme, crushed
- 1 teaspoon poultry seasoning
- ¾ teaspoon salt
- ½ teaspoon pepper
- 5½ cups water
- ½ cup dairy sour cream

1. Combine uncooked wild rice, uncooked brown rice, soup, mushrooms, carrots, celery, onion, apricots, thyme, poultry seasoning, salt, and pepper in a 3½- or 4-quart slow cooker. Stir in water.

2. Cover; cook on low-heat setting for 7 to 8 hours or on high-heat setting for 3½ to 4 hours. Stir in sour cream and serve.

Per serving: 165 cal., 4 g total fat (2 g sat. fat), 4 mg chol., 339 mg sodium, 28 g carb., 2 g fiber, 4 g pro.

California Vegetable Casserole

This cheesy vegetable-rice combo is terrific for toting to potluck suppers.

Prep: 15 minutes
Cook: 4½ to 5½ hours (low)
Makes 6 servings

- 1 16-ounce package loose-pack frozen California-blend vegetables (cauliflower, broccoli, and carrots)
- 1 10¾-ounce can condensed cream of mushroom soup
- 1 cup instant white rice
- ½ of a 15-ounce jar (about 1 cup) processed cheese dip
- ⅔ cup milk
- ⅓ cup chopped onion
- ¼ cup water
- 2 tablespoons butter, cut up

1. Place frozen vegetables in a 3½- to 4-quart slow cooker. In a small bowl combine soup, uncooked rice, cheese dip, milk, onion, water, and butter. Pour over the vegetables.

2. Cover; cook on low-heat setting for 4½ to 5½ hours or until vegetables and rice are tender. Stir before serving.

Per serving: 292 cal., 17 g total fat (10 g sat. fat), 36 mg chol., 1,124 mg sodium, 26 g carb., 3 g fiber, 9 g pro.

Maple-Ginger Sweet Potatoes

When baked ham, pork roast, or **holiday** turkey is on the menu, cook a batch of these **cranberry- and apple-kissed** sweet potatoes to spoon alongside.

Maple-Ginger Sweet Potatoes

Light syrup adds just enough sweetness to bring out the best in the sweet potatoes, apples, and cranberries.
Prep: 25 minutes
Cook: 5 to 6 hours (low) or 2½ to 3 hours (high)
Makes 8 servings

1½	pounds sweet potatoes, peeled and cut into bite-size pieces (about 5 cups)
2	medium tart cooking apples (such as Granny Smith), cored and coarsely chopped (about 2 cups)
¼	cup dried cranberries, snipped
1½	teaspoons grated fresh ginger
½	teaspoon salt
½	teaspoon ground cinnamon
¼	teaspoon ground nutmeg
⅛	teaspoon ground black pepper
½	cup water
¼	cup light pancake and waffle syrup product

1. In a 3½- or 4-quart slow cooker, combine sweet potatoes, apples, dried cranberries, ginger, salt, cinnamon, nutmeg, and pepper. Pour the water and syrup over all.

2. Cover and cook on low-heat setting for 5 to 6 hours or on high-heat setting for 2½ to 3 hours.

Per serving: 92 cal., 0 g total fat (0 g sat. fat), 0 mg chol., 194 mg sodium, 23 g carb., 3 g fiber, 1 g pro.

Spicy Creamed Corn

If you like spicy foods, kick this corn up a notch by using Monterey Jack cheese with jalapeño chile peppers.
Prep: 15 minutes
Cook: 5 to 6 hours (low) or 2½ to 3 hours (high)
Stand: 10 minutes
Makes 12 servings

2	16-ounce packages frozen white whole kernel corn (shoepeg), thawed
1	14¾-ounce can cream-style corn
2	cups shredded Monterey Jack cheese (8 ounces)
1	cup chopped tomato
⅓	cup chopped onion
1	4½-ounce can diced green chile peppers, undrained
1½	teaspoons chili powder
½	teaspoon salt
1	16-ounce carton dairy sour cream
2	tablespoons snipped fresh cilantro

1. In a 3½- or 4-quart slow cooker, combine thawed whole kernel corn, cream-style corn, shredded cheese, tomato, onion, undrained chile peppers, chili powder, and salt.

2. Cover and cook on low-heat setting for 5 to 6 hours or on high-heat setting for 2½ to 3 hours.

3. Gently stir in sour cream and cilantro. Let stand for 10 minutes before serving.

Per serving: 250 cal., 15 g total fat (9 g sat. fat), 33 mg chol., 350 mg sodium, 25 g carb., 2 g fiber, 9 g pro.

Easy Cheesy Potatoes

Balsamic Root Vegetables

Root vegetables and balsamic vinegar are a **popular** side dish often served at the **trendiest** restaurants. Bring the **flavors** home to your slow cooker with this **easy-to-prepare** recipe.

Wild Rice with Pecans and Cherries

Wild Rice with Pecans and Cherries

If you've been invited to a "turkey and all the trimmings" potluck dinner, help out with the trimmings by bringing this elegant rice pilaf.

Prep: 20 minutes
Cook: 5 to 6 hours (low)
Stand: 10 minutes
Makes 15 servings

3	14-ounce cans chicken broth
2½	cups wild rice, rinsed and drained
1	cup coarsely shredded carrot
1	4½-ounce jar (drained weight) sliced mushrooms, drained
2	tablespoons butter or margarine, melted
2	teaspoons dried marjoram, crushed
¼	teaspoon salt
¼	teaspoon ground black pepper
⅔	cup dried tart cherries
⅔	cup chopped green onions
½	cup coarsely chopped pecans, toasted
	Chopped green onions (optional)

1. In a 3½- or 4-quart slow cooker, combine broth, uncooked wild rice, carrot, mushrooms, melted butter, marjoram, salt, and pepper.

2. Cover and cook on low-heat setting for 5 to 6 hours.

3. Turn off cooker. Stir in dried cherries, the ⅔ cup green onions, and the pecans. Cover and let stand for 10 minutes. Serve with a slotted spoon. If desired, garnish with additional green onions.

Per serving: 169 cal., 5 g total fat (1 g sat. fat), 4 mg chol., 423 mg sodium, 27 g carb., 3 g fiber, 5 g pro.

Pineapple-Peach Cobbler

Pineapple and peaches simmer into a mellow fruit filling that's scrumptious beneath fluffy iced cinnamon rolls.

Prep: 15 minutes
Cook: 1½ hours (high), plus 1 hour
Stand: 30 minutes
Makes 8 servings

Nonstick cooking spray
2 21-ounce cans pineapple pie filling
1 6- or 7-ounce package dried peaches, snipped
½ cup orange juice
1 17½-ounce package (5) refrigerated large cinnamon rolls
Vanilla ice cream (optional)

1. Lightly coat a 3½- or 4-quart slow cooker with cooking spray. In the prepared cooker, combine pie filling, dried peaches, and orange juice.

2. Cover and cook on high-heat setting about 1½ hours or until fruit mixture is hot and bubbly.

3. Stir fruit mixture. Place cinnamon rolls on a cutting board, cinnamon sides up (set icing aside). Cut each roll in half to make two semicircles. Place roll halves on top of fruit mixture in cooker, cinnamon sides up.

4. Cover and cook about 1 hour more or until rolls are fluffy all the way through.

5. Remove liner from cooker, if possible, or turn off cooker. Let stand, uncovered, for 30 to 45 minutes to cool slightly before serving. Spread icing over rolls. If desired, top individual servings with ice cream.
Per serving: 467 cal., 8 g total fat (2 g sat. fat), 0 mg chol., 493 mg sodium, 96 g carb., 2 g fiber, 4 g pro.

Hot German-Style Potato Salad

This slow-cooker version of the old-world favorite is ideal for when the whole family gets together. Stirring in the bacon just before serving helps keep it crisp.

Prep: 25 minutes
Cook: 8 to 9 hours (low) or 4 to 4½ hours (high)
Makes 8 servings

6 cups peeled potatoes, cut into ¾-inch cubes
1 cup chopped onion
1 cup water
⅔ cup cider vinegar
¼ cup sugar
2 tablespoons quick-cooking tapioca
1 teaspoon salt
¼ teaspoon celery seeds
¼ teaspoon ground black pepper
6 slices bacon, crisp-cooked, drained, and crumbled

1. In a 3½- or 4-quart slow cooker, combine potatoes and onion. In a medium bowl, combine the water, cider vinegar, sugar, tapioca, salt, celery seeds, and pepper; pour over potatoes in cooker.

2. Cover and cook on low-heat setting for 8 to 9 hours or on high-heat setting for 4 to 4½ hours. Stir in bacon.
Per serving: 160 cal., 2 g total fat (1 g sat. fat), 4 mg chol., 374 mg sodium, 32 g carb., 2 g fiber, 4 g pro.

Mock Cherries Jubilee

Mock Cherries Jubilee

Prep: 15 minutes
Cook: 4 to 5 hours (high)
Makes 8 servings

- 2 **16-ounce packages frozen unsweetened pitted tart red cherries**
- ½ **cup cherry cider, apple cider, or apple juice**
- ½ **cup packed brown sugar**
- 2 **tablespoons quick-cooking tapioca**
- 1 **vanilla bean, split lengthwise, or 2 teaspoons vanilla**
- 2 **to 3 tablespoons cherry or almond liqueur**
  Pound cake slices, angel food cake slices, or vanilla ice cream
  Whipped cream (optional)

1. In a 3½- or 4-quart slow cooker combine frozen cherries, cider, brown sugar, tapioca, and vanilla bean, if using.

2. Cover; cook on high-heat setting for 4 to 5 hours. Remove and discard vanilla bean halves, if using, or stir in vanilla. Stir in cherry or almond liqueur. Spoon over cake slices or ice cream in bowls. If desired, top with whipped cream.

Per serving: 428 cal., 15 g total fat (9 g sat. fat), 166 mg chol., 307 mg sodium, 68 g carb., 2 g fiber, 5 g pro.

Crockery Dressing

When the oven is full, and you don't want to prepare the stuffing in the turkey, fix this slow-cooked version.
Prep: 10 minutes
Cook: 4 to 5 hours (low)
Makes 8 to 10 servings

- 12 **cups dry bread cubes**
- 2 **cups sliced celery**
- ½ **cup finely chopped onion**
- ¼ **cup snipped fresh parsley**
- 1½ **teaspoons dried sage, crushed**
- ½ **teaspoon dried marjoram, crushed**
- ¼ **teaspoon pepper**
- 1½ **cups chicken broth**
- ¼ **cup margarine or butter, melted**

1. In a large bowl combine the dry bread cubes, celery, onion, parsley, sage, marjoram, and pepper.

2. Pour chicken broth and margarine or butter over bread mixture and toss gently. Place bread mixture in a 3½-, 4-, or 5-quart crockery cooker.

3. Cover; cook on low-heat setting for 4 to 5 hours.

Per serving: 253 cal., 9 g total fat (2 g sat. fat), 0 mg chol., 568 mg sodium, 37 g carb., g fiber, 7 g pro.

Multigrain Pilaf

At the supermarket you may find frozen sweet soybeans sold under their Japanese name, edamame.

Prep: 20 minutes
Cook: 6 to 8 hours (low) or 3 to 4 hours (high)
Makes 12 servings

⅔	cup wheat berries
½	cup regular barley
½	cup wild rice
2	14-ounce cans vegetable broth or chicken broth
2	cups loose-pack frozen sweet soybeans (edamame) or baby lima beans
1	medium red sweet pepper, chopped
1	medium onion, finely chopped
1	tablespoon butter or margarine
¾	teaspoon dried sage, crushed
½	teaspoon salt
¼	teaspoon coarsely ground black pepper
4	cloves garlic, minced

1. Rinse and drain wheat berries, barley, and wild rice. In a 3½- or 4-quart slow cooker, combine uncooked wheat berries, uncooked barley, uncooked wild rice, broth, soybeans, sweet pepper, onion, butter, sage, salt, black pepper, and garlic.

2. Cover and cook on low-heat setting for 6 to 8 hours or on high-heat setting for 3 to 4 hours. Stir before serving.

Per serving: 169 cal., 4 g total fat (1 g sat. fat), 3 mg chol., 386 mg sodium, 25 g carb., 5 g fiber, 9 g pro.

Double-Berry Cobbler

Prep: 25 minutes
Cook: 1¾ to 2 hours (high)
Stand: 1 hour
Makes 6 servings

1	cup all-purpose flour
1¾	cup sugar
1	teaspoon baking powder
¼	teaspoon salt
¼	teaspoon ground cinnamon
¼	teaspoon ground nutmeg
2	eggs
3	tablespoons cooking oil
2	tablespoons milk
3	cups fresh blueberries or one 16-ounce bag frozen blueberries
3	cups fresh blackberries or one 16-ounce bag frozen blackberries
1	cup water
3	tablespoons quick-cooking tapioca
	Vanilla ice cream (optional)

1. In a medium bowl, stir together flour, the ¾ cup of the sugar, the baking powder, salt, cinnamon, and nutmeg. In a small bowl, beat eggs with a fork; stir in oil and milk. Add egg mixture to flour mixture; stir just until moistened. Set batter aside.

2. In a large saucepan, combine blueberries, blackberries, the 1 cup remaining sugar, the water, and tapioca. Bring to boiling. Pour mixture into a 3½- or 4-quart slow cooker. Immediately spoon batter over mixture.

3. Cover and cook on high-heat setting for 1¾ to 2 hours or until a toothpick inserted into the center of the topper comes out clean. Remove liner from cooker, if possible, or turn off cooker. Let stand for 1 hour to cool slightly before serving. If desired, serve with ice cream.

Per serving: 478 cal., 10 g total fat (2 g sat. fat), 71 mg chol., 194 mg sodium, 97 g carb., 6 g fiber, 6 g pro.

Multigrain Pilaf

Wheat berries, barley, and **wild rice** combine
for a dish that is wholesome, filling, and **infinitely
interesting.** Pair the pilaf with your favorite
roasted or grilled **meats.**

Curry powder, coconut milk, and a sprinkling of fresh **basil** make this medley of cauliflower, garbanzo beans, **green beans,** and carrot rich and **full-flavored.**

Vegetable and Garbanzo Curry

Nutty Mocha Pudding Cake

Chocolate lovers won't be able to resist this nutty double-chocolate cake oozing with warm pudding.

Prep: 20 minutes
Cook: 2½ hours (high)
Stand: 30 minutes
Makes 8 servings

  1   cup all-purpose flour
1¼   cups sugar
  2   tablespoons unsweetened cocoa powder
1½   teaspoons baking powder
  ½   cup milk
  2   tablespoons butter, melted
  1   teaspoon vanilla
  ½   cup miniature semisweet chocolate pieces
  ½   cup broken pecans
  ¼   cup unsweetened cocoa powder
  1   tablespoon instant coffee crystals
  ¼   cup coffee liqueur (optional)

1. In a medium bowl, stir together flour, the ½ cup of the sugar, the 2 tablespoons cocoa powder, and the baking powder. Add milk, melted butter, and vanilla. Stir until batter is smooth. Stir in chocolate pieces and pecans. Spread batter evenly in the bottom of a 3½- or 4-quart slow cooker.

2. In a small bowl, combine the remaining ¾ cup sugar and the ¼ cup cocoa powder. Dissolve coffee crystals in 1½ cups boiling water; if desired, stir in coffee liqueur. Gradually stir coffee mixture into the sugar-cocoa mixture. Pour evenly over batter in cooker.

3. Cover and cook on high-heat setting for 2½ hours (center may appear moist, but will set up upon standing). Turn off cooker. Let stand for 30 minutes to cool slightly before serving. To serve, spoon warm cake into dessert dishes; spoon pudding over cake.

Per serving: 487 cal., 20 g total fat (10 g sat. fat), 38 mg chol., 169 mg sodium, 1 g carb., 1 g fiber, 7 g pro.

Vegetable and Garbanzo Curry

You'll find coconut milk in the Asian food section of larger supermarkets or at Asian food specialty stores.

Prep: 25 minutes
Cook: 5 to 6 hours (low) or 2½ to 3 hours (high)
Makes 4 to 6 servings

  3   cups cauliflower florets
  1   15-ounce can garbanzo beans (chickpeas), rinsed and drained
  1   cup loose-pack frozen cut green beans
  1   cup sliced carrot
  ½   cup chopped onion
  1   14-ounce can vegetable broth
  2   to 3 teaspoons curry powder
  1   14-ounce can light coconut milk
  ¼   cup shredded fresh basil leaves

1. In a 3½- or 4-quart slow cooker, combine cauliflower, garbanzo beans, frozen green beans, carrot, and onion. Stir in broth and curry powder.

2. Cover and cook on low-heat setting for 5 to 6 hours or on high-heat setting for 2½ to 3 hours. Stir in coconut milk and basil.

Per serving: 219 cal., 7 g total fat (4 g sat. fat), 0 mg chol., 805 mg sodium, 32 g carb., 9 g fiber, 8 g pro.

What's a Chiffonade?

The French word for the shredded basil used in Vegetable and Garbanzo Curry is chiffonade or "made of rags." The easiest way to shred basil, or to make a chiffonade using any leafy fresh herb or green, is to wind the leaves into a tight roll, then cut the rolls into thin slices.

Saucy Succotash

Having a cookout? Serve this cheesy medley along with burgers and brats.

Prep: 15 minutes
Cook: 5 to 6 hours (low) or 2½ to 3 hours (high)
Stand: 10 minutes
Makes 12 servings

1   **16-ounce package frozen whole kernel corn, thawed**
1   **16-ounce package frozen lima beans, thawed**
1   **14¾-ounce can cream-style corn**
1   **cup chopped red sweet pepper**
1   **cup shredded smoked Gouda cheese (4 ounces)**
½   **cup chopped onion**
2   **teaspoons cumin seeds**
¼   **cup water**
1   **8-ounce carton light dairy sour cream**

1. In a 3½- or 4-quart slow cooker, combine whole kernel corn, lima beans, cream-style corn, sweet pepper, cheese, onion, and cumin seeds. Pour the water over all.

2. Cover and cook on low-heat setting for 5 to 6 hours or on high-heat setting for 2½ to 3 hours.

3. Gently stir in sour cream. Let stand for 10 minutes before serving.

Per serving: 158 cal., 4 g total fat (3 g sat. fat), 14 mg chol., 282 mg sodium, 25 g carb., 4 g fiber, 7 g pro.

Apple Betty

Now this is comfort food—apples and apple butter simmered with brown sugar and cinnamon-raisin bread!

Prep: 25 minutes
Cook: 4 hours (low)
Stand: 30 minutes
Makes 6 to 8 servings

   Nonstick cooking spray
5   **tart cooking apples, peeled, cored, and sliced (5 cups)**
¾   **cup packed brown sugar**
⅔   **cup apple butter**
½   **cup water**
5   **cups soft cinnamon-raisin bread cut into ½-inch cubes (about 5 slices)**
⅓   **cup butter, melted**
   Caramel ice cream topping and/or vanilla ice cream (optional)

1. Lightly coat a 3½- or 4-quart slow cooker with cooking spray; set aside.

2. In a large bowl, combine apples, brown sugar, apple butter, and the water. Toss until apples are coated. Place bread cubes in a medium bowl. Drizzle with melted butter, tossing until mixed.

3. Place half of the buttered bread cubes in prepared cooker. Pour all of the apple mixture over bread cubes. Sprinkle remaining bread cubes over the apple mixture in cooker.

4. Cover and cook on low-heat setting for 4 hours.

5. Remove liner from cooker, if possible, or turn off cooker. Let stand, uncovered, for 30 minutes to cool slightly before serving. If desired, top individual servings with caramel ice cream topping and/or vanilla ice cream.

Per serving: 492 cal., 12 g total fat (7 g sat. fat), 29 mg chol., 209 mg sodium, 97 g carb., 5 g fiber, 2 g pro.

Saucy Succotash

Two kinds of corn, lima beans, and sweet pepper dressed with a **generous** helping of **smoked Gouda** cheese and plenty of **sour cream** make a terrific side dish.

quick **desserts**

Cap off a carefree slow-cooked meal with one of these equally no-fuss desserts. They take almost no time to prepare, yet are oh-so scrumptious.

Warm Apple Spice Crumble
Makes 4 servings

Preheat oven to 375°F. In a 2-quart square baking dish, combine one 20-ounce can sliced apples (undrained) and 1/4 cup golden raisins or mixed dried fruit bits. Stir in 1 teaspoon vanilla. Sprinkle 2 to 3 tablespoons sugar and 1 teaspoon apple pie spice or ground cinnamon over apple mixture. Top with 3 tablespoons butter, cut into small pieces. Sprinkle 1 1/2 cups low-fat granola and 1/4 cup flaked coconut evenly over apple mixture. Bake for 12 to 15 minutes or until apples are heated through and topping is golden. Serve warm. If desired, top individual servings with vanilla ice cream.

Per serving: 423 cal., 14 g total fat (8 g sat. fat), 23 mg chol., 188 mg sodium, 74 g carb., 6 g fiber, 5 g pro.

Crunchy Pound Cake Slices
Makes 4 servings

Preheat broiler. Place four 1/2-inch-thick slices pound cake on a cookie sheet. Broil 3 to 4 inches from heat about 2 minutes or until lightly browned, turning once. Cool slightly. Using 1/4 cup chocolate hazelnut spread, spread one side of each cake slice with 1 tablespoon of the spread. Sprinkle each slice with 2 tablespoons roasted mixed nuts, coarsely chopped; pat gently to form an even layer. Transfer each slice to a dessert plate; top with a scoop of caramel or cinnamon ice cream. Serve immediately.

Per serving: 763 cal., 45 g total fat (22 g sat. fat), 206 mg chol., 421 mg sodium, 82 g carb., 2 g fiber, 12 g pro.

Dessert Waffles
Makes 6 servings

Press one 10-ounce package frozen raspberries in syrup, thawed, through a fine-mesh sieve; discard seeds. In a small bowl, combine sieved berries and 1/4 cup sifted powdered sugar.

Toast 6 frozen waffles; cut each diagonally in half. For each serving, top two waffle halves with 1/2 cup vanilla ice cream and some of the raspberry mixture.

Per serving: 361 cal., 15 g total fat (8 g sat. fat), 79 mg chol., 381 mg sodium, 54 g carb., 2 g fiber, 5 g pro.

Mango Whip
Makes 4 servings

Seed and peel 4 mangoes or peaches. Cut into wedges. Divide fruit among four dessert dishes.

In a small bowl, beat together 4 ounces reduced-fat cream cheese (Neufchâtel), softened, and 1/4 cup white grape or orange juice. Spoon over fruit. Top each serving with 1 tablespoon chopped pistachios.

Per serving: 263 cal., 11 g total fat (5 g sat. fat), 22 mg chol., 118 mg sodium, 41 g carb., 5 g fiber, 6 g pro

Warm Citrus Fruit with Brown Sugar
Makes 4 servings

Preheat broiler. Peel and section 2 medium red grapefruit* and 2 medium oranges. In a medium bowl, combine grapefruit, oranges, and 1 cup fresh pineapple chunks or one 8-ounce can pineapple chunks, drained. Transfer to a 1-quart broiler-safe au gratin dish or casserole.

In a small bowl, stir together ¼ cup packed brown sugar and 2 tablespoons softened butter until well mixed; sprinkle over fruit. Broil about 4 inches from the heat for 5 to 6 minutes or until sugar is bubbly and fruit is warmed.

Per serving: 192 cal., 6 g total fat (4 g sat. fat), 16 mg chol., 68 mg sodium, 35 g carb., 4 g fiber, 2 g pro.

*Note: If you prefer, use 1½ cups refrigerated grapefruit sections, drained, rather than fresh grapefruit sections.

Cherry Dream
Makes 4 servings

Divide 2 cups pitted halved fresh dark sweet cherries or 2 cups frozen dark sweet cherries, thawed, halved, and drained, among four chilled dessert dishes.

Prepare one 4-serving-size package vanilla or lemon instant pudding mix according to package directions. Spoon prepared pudding over cherries. (Or spoon four individual vanilla or lemon pudding cups over cherries.) If desired, drizzle each serving with 1 tablespoon cherry liqueur, such as Kirsch.

Per serving: 196 cal., 3 g total fat (2 g sat. fat), 10 mg chol., 410 mg sodium, 41 g carb., 2 g fiber, 5 g pro.

Keen Nectarines
Makes 6 servings

Divide 1 pint (2 cups) vanilla or peach-flavor frozen yogurt (or vanilla or peach-flavor ice cream) among six chilled dessert bowls.

Add half of a pitted ripe nectarine or peach to each bowl. Crumble 6 amaretti cookies or gingersnaps. Sprinkle the crumbled cookies over fruit and frozen yogurt.

Per serving: 132 cal., 3 g total fat (1 g sat. fat), 7 mg chol., 24 mg sodium, 25 g carb., 1 g fiber, 3 g pro.

Crock of Reubens

party foods

The next time you're hosting a party, wow everyone with one or more of these fabulous no-tend slow-cooker dishes. They stay warm and inviting for hours, leaving you free to mingle with your guests and have a great time.

Crock of Reubens

If your favorite bakery doesn't routinely carry mini buns, ask them to make some for you.

Prep: 20 minutes   **Cook:** 4 to 6 hours (low) or 2 to 3 hours (high)
Makes 24 sandwiches

- 1   **2- to 3-pound corned beef brisket with spice packet**
- 1   **16-ounce jar sauerkraut, drained**
- ½   **cup bottled Thousand Island salad dressing**
- 24 **small rye or whole wheat rolls, split and toasted**
- 2   **cups shredded Swiss cheese (8 ounces)**
  Bottled Thousand Island salad dressing (optional)

1. Trim fat from meat. If necessary, cut meat to fit into a 3½- or 4-quart slow cooker. Place meat in cooker. Sprinkle with spices from packet. Spread sauerkraut over the meat. Drizzle the ½ cup salad dressing over all.

2. Cover and cook on low-heat setting for 4 to 6 hours or on high-heat setting for 2 to 3 hours.

3. Remove meat from cooker and place on cutting board. Thinly slice meat against the grain. Return sliced meat to the cooker; stir to combine with the cooking liquid.

4. Using a slotted spoon, spoon corned beef mixture onto toasted rolls. Top with cheese and, if desired, additional salad dressing. If desired, secure with cocktail picks.

Per sandwich: 231 cal., 13 g total fat (5 g sat. fat), 47 mg chol., 1,165 mg sodium, 17 g carb., 3 g fiber, 12 g pro.

Party Foods to Go

When the party's not at your place but you'd like to help with the refreshments, warm appetizers simmered in a slow cooker are a tasty solution. Prepare the appetizer according to recipe directions. Once the food is cooked, wrap the slow cooker in several layers of newspaper or a thick towel. Then place it in an insulated container to transport it. When you arrive at the party, promptly plug in your slow cooker. Don't leave food in an unplugged slow cooker for more than 2 hours.

Five-Spice Chicken Wings

Five-spice powder is often found in Asian-inspired dishes such as these tangy appetizer wings. The spice incorporates the **five basic flavors** of Chinese cooking—sweet, sour, bitter, savory, and salty.

Five-Spice Chicken Wings

Prep: 20 minutes
Bake: 20 minutes
Cook: 4 to 5 hours (low) or 2 to 2½ hours (high)
Makes 16 servings

- 3 **pounds chicken wings (about 16)**
- 1 **cup bottled plum sauce**
- 2 **tablespoons butter, melted**
- 1 **teaspoon five-spice powder**
  Thin orange wedges and pineapple slices (optional)

1. If desired, use a sharp knife to carefully cut off tips of the wings; discard wing tips. In a foil-lined 15×10×1-inch shallow baking pan arrange wing pieces in a single layer. Bake in a 375°F oven for 20 minutes. Drain well.

2. For sauce, in a 3½- or 4-quart slow cooker combine plum sauce, melted butter, and five-spice powder. Add wing pieces, stirring to coat with sauce.

3. Cover; cook on low-heat setting for 4 to 5 hours or on high-heat setting for 2 to 2½ hours.

4. Serve immediately or keep covered on low-heat setting for up to 2 hours. If desired, garnish with orange wedges and pineapple slices.

Per serving: 88 cal., 6 g total fat (2 g sat. fat), 35 mg chol., 41 mg sodium, 3 g carb., 0 g fiber, 6 g pro.

Kentucky Chicken Wings: Prepare chicken as in Step 1. For sauce, in slow cooker combine ½ cup maple syrup, ½ cup whiskey, and 2 tablespoons melted butter. Add wing pieces, stirring to coat with sauce. Continue as in Step 3.

Buffalo-Style Chicken Wings: Prepare chicken as in Step 1. For sauce, in slow cooker combine 1½ cups hot-style barbecue sauce, 2 tablespoons melted butter, and 1 to 2 teaspoons bottled hot pepper sauce. Add wing pieces, stirring to coat with sauce. Continue as in Step 3. Serve with bottled blue cheese or ranch salad dressing. Omit the fruit garnish.

Super Simple Bean Dip

Few hot party dips are easier—and few will disappear more quickly— than this fantastic, four-ingredient crowd-pleaser.

Prep: 10 minutes
Cook: 3½ to 4 hours (low)
Makes 22 servings

- 2 **16-ounce cans refried beans**
- 1 **11-ounce can condensed nacho cheese soup**
- ½ **cup bottled salsa**
- ¼ **cup sliced green onions**
  Tortilla chips

1. In a 1½-quart slow cooker combine refried beans, nacho cheese soup, and salsa. Cover and cook on low-heat setting for 3½ to 4 hours.

2. Sprinkle with green onions. Serve dip with tortilla chips.

Per serving (dip only): 53 cal., 1 g total fat (0 g sat. fat), 2 mg chol., 330 mg sodium, 8 g carb., 2 g fiber, 3 g pro.

Five-Spice Pecans

When you have some of these lively nuts left over, sprinkle them on salads or serve them with fresh pear slices for dessert.

Prep: 10 minutes
Cook: 2 hours (low)
Makes 4 cups

1	**pound pecan halves, toasted* (4 cups)**
¼	**cup butter or margarine, melted**
2	**tablespoons soy sauce**
1	**teaspoon five-spice powder**
½	**teaspoon garlic powder**
½	**teaspoon ground ginger**
¼	**teaspoon cayenne pepper**

1. Place toasted pecans in a 3½- or 4-quart slow cooker. In a small bowl, combine melted butter, soy sauce, five-spice powder, garlic powder, ginger, and cayenne pepper. Pour butter mixture over nuts in cooker; stir to coat.

2. Cover and cook on low-heat setting for 2 hours.

3. Stir nuts. Spread nuts in a single layer on waxed paper to cool. (Nuts will appear soft after cooking, but will crisp upon cooling.) Store in a tightly covered container for up to 2 weeks.

Per ¼ cup: 225 cal., 23 g total fat (4 g sat. fat), 8 mg chol., 146 mg sodium, 4 g carb., 3 g fiber, 3 g pro.

*Note: To toast pecans, preheat oven to 350°F. Spread pecans in a single layer on a shallow baking pan. Bake for 5 to 10 minutes or until toasted, stirring once so nuts don't burn.

Mexican-Style Meatballs and Mini Sausages

The hotter the salsa you use, the more firepower these saucy meat tidbits will have.

Prep: 25 minutes
Bake: 18 minutes
Cook: 3 to 4 hours (low) or 1½ to 2 hours (high)
Makes 20 servings

1	**egg**
¼	**cup fine dry bread crumbs**
¼	**cup finely chopped onion**
3	**cloves garlic, minced**
12	**ounces lean ground beef**
4	**ounces uncooked chorizo sausage (remove casing, if present)**
1	**16-ounce jar salsa**
1	**12-ounce jar chili sauce**
1	**16-ounce package small cooked smoked sausage links**
2	**tablespoons snipped fresh cilantro (optional)**

1. Preheat oven to 350°F. In a medium bowl, beat egg with a fork; stir in bread crumbs, onion, and garlic. Add ground beef and chorizo sausage; mix well. Shape into about thirty-eight 1-inch meatballs.

2. Place meatballs in a 15×10×1-inch baking pan. Bake about 18 minutes or until meatballs are cooked through. Drain off fat. Pat dry with paper towels.

3. In a 3½- or 4-quart slow cooker, stir together salsa and chili sauce. Stir in baked meatballs and smoked sausage links. Cook on low-heat setting for 3 to 4 hours or on high-heat setting for 1½ to 2 hours. If desired, sprinkle with cilantro before serving. Serve with decorative wooden picks.

Per serving: 156 cal., 10 g total fat (4 g sat. fat), 41 mg chol., 708 mg sodium, 7 g carb., 1 g fiber, 9 g pro.

Bite-size meatballs made with a mix of ground beef and chorizo simmer with tiny smoked sausages in this tongue-tingling south-of-the-border-style appetizer.

Mexican-Style Meatballs and Mini Sausages

Cheesy Beer-Salsa Dip

Serve this hot dip with dippers made of something unexpected—corn bread. The crunchy sticks are a nice contrast to the spicy dip.

Prep: 15 minutes
Cook: 3 to 4 hours (low) or 1½ to 2 hours (high)
Makes 22 (¼-cup) servings

1   **16-ounce jar salsa**
⅔   **cup beer or milk**
4   **cups shredded American cheese (1 pound)**
2   **cups shredded Monterey Jack cheese (8 ounces)**
1   **8-ounce package cream cheese, cut up**
    Corn Bread Dippers or tortilla chips

1. In a 3½- or 4-quart slow cooker, combine salsa and beer, add American cheese, Monterey Jack cheese, and cream cheese.

2. Cover and cook on low-heat setting for 3 to 4 hours or on high-heat setting for 1½ to 2 hours. Serve immediately or keep covered on low-heat setting for up to 2 hours. Stir just before serving. Serve with Corn Bread Dippers or tortilla chips.

Per serving (dip only): 211 cal., 15 g total fat (8 g sat. fat), 47 mg chol., 557 mg sodium, 10 g carb., 0 g fiber, 9 g pro.

Corn Bread Dippers: Preheat oven to 400°F. Prepare one 8½-ounce package corn muffin mix according to package directions. Spread batter in an 8x8x2-inch baking pan. Bake about 20 minutes or until a wooden toothpick inserted in the center comes out clean. Cool bread in pan on a wire rack for 5 minutes. Remove bread from pan; cool completely. Preheat oven to 425°F. Cut into ½-inch-thick slices; cut each slice into 3 pieces. Place in a single layer on a large baking sheet. Bake about 10 minutes more or until crisp, turning once. Cool on a wire rack.

Make-Ahead Directions: Prepare Corn Bread Dippers as directed. Cool sticks completely and store, covered, in an airtight container for up to 2 days.

Hot Buttered Cider

The little dab of butter floating on top of each cup makes this hot drink as smooth and comforting as a soft sweater.

Prep: 10 minutes
Cook: 4 to 6 hours (low) or 2 to 3 hours (high)
Makes 12 (about 8-ounce) servings

4   **inches stick cinnamon, broken into 1-inch pieces**
1   **teaspoon whole allspice**
1   **teaspoon whole cloves**
    Peel from 1 lemon, cut into strips
8   **cups apple cider or apple juice**
2   **tablespoons packed brown sugar**
2   **tablespoons butter**

1. For spice bag, cut a double thickness of 100-percent-cotton cheesecloth into a 6-inch square. Place cinnamon, allspice, cloves, and lemon peel in center of cloth. Bring corners together and tie with a clean string. In a 3½- or 4-quart slow cooker combine spice bag, apple cider, and brown sugar.

2. Cover; cook on low-heat setting for 4 to 6 hours or on high-heat setting 2 to 3 hours.

3. Remove spice bag; discard. Serve immediately or keep covered on low-heat setting for up to 2 hours. Ladle cider into mugs. Top each serving with ½ teaspoon butter.

Per serving: 101 cal., 2 g total fat (1 g sat. fat), 5 mg chol., 26 mg sodium, 21 g carb., 0 g fiber, 0 g pro.

To serve a crowd: Place 6 inches of stick cinnamon (broken into 1-inch pieces), 1½ teaspoons whole allspice, 1½ teaspoons whole cloves and the peel from 1 large lemon in center of cloth as in Step 1. In a 5½- or 6-quart slow cooker combine spice bag, 16 cups apple cider, and ¼ cup packed brown sugar. Continue as in Step 2. Top each serving with ½ teaspoon butter (¼ cup butter total). Makes 24 servings.

Cheesy Beer-Salsa Dip

Picadillo Dip

Hot and Peppery Turkey Sandwiches

Liquid smoke gives the tender turkey just-off-the-grill flavor, while the coleslaw adds a captivating crunch.

Prep: 25 minutes
Cook: 10 to 12 hours (low) or 5 to 6 hours (high), plus 15 minutes on low
Makes 24 sandwiches

3	pounds turkey thighs, skinned
½	cup packed brown sugar
¼	cup yellow mustard
2	tablespoons ketchup
2	tablespoons cider vinegar
1	tablespoon quick-cooking tapioca
2	teaspoons liquid smoke
1	teaspoon salt
1	teaspoon coarsely ground black pepper
1	teaspoon crushed red pepper
24	miniature hamburger buns, split and toasted
1	cup deli coleslaw

1. Place turkey thighs in a 3½- or 4-quart slow cooker. In a small bowl, combine brown sugar, mustard, ketchup, vinegar, tapioca, liquid smoke, salt, black pepper, and crushed red pepper. Pour over turkey in cooker.

2. Cover and cook on low-heat setting for 10 to 12 hours or on high-heat setting for 5 to 6 hours.

3. Remove turkey from cooker, reserving cooking juices. Using two forks, pull turkey off bones and into shreds; discard bones. Skim fat from cooking juices. Return turkey to cooker. If using high-heat setting, turn to low-heat setting. Cover and cook for 15 to 30 minutes more or until heated through.

4. Serve turkey mixture on hamburger buns. Top with coleslaw.

Per sandwich: 183 cal., 4 g total fat (1 g sat. fat), 38 mg chol., 315 mg sodium, 25 g carb., 1 g fiber, 10 g pro.

Picadillo Dip

Picadillo is usually a mix of garlic, onion, tomatoes, and meat, but this version mingles in olives, almonds, and raisins for a sophisticated twist.

Prep: 20 minutes
Cook: 6 to 8 hours (low) or 3 to 4 hours (high)
Makes 4 cups

1	pound ground beef
1	16-ounce jar salsa
1	medium onion, chopped
½	cup raisins
¼	cup sliced pimiento-stuffed olives
2	tablespoons red wine vinegar
3	cloves garlic, minced
½	teaspoon ground cinnamon
½	teaspoon ground cumin
¼	cup slivered almonds, toasted
	Slivered almonds, toasted (optional)
	Toasted pita wedges or bagel chips

1. In a large skillet, cook meat until brown. Drain off fat. In a 3½- or 4-quart slow cooker, stir together meat, salsa, onion, raisins, olives, red wine vinegar, garlic, cinnamon, and cumin.

2. Cover and cook on low-heat setting for 6 to 8 hours or on high-heat setting for 3 to 4 hours.

3. Stir the ¼ cup almonds into mixture in cooker. If desired, sprinkle with additional almonds. Serve with toasted pita wedges.

Per ¼ cup dip: 94 cal., 5 g total fat (2 g sat. fat), 18 mg chol., 217 mg sodium, 7 g carb., 1 g fiber, 7 g pro.

Cajun Spinach-Shrimp Dip

*Treat your guests to something sensational—
serve them this spicy Louisiana-style shrimp dip.*

Prep: 15 minutes
Cook: 2 to 3 hours (low)
Makes 12 (¼ cup) servings

- 1   10¾-ounce can condensed cream of shrimp or cream of chicken soup
- 1   10-ounce package frozen chopped spinach, thawed and well drained
- 1   8-ounce package cream cheese, cubed
- 1   4-ounce can tiny shrimp, drained
- ¼   cup finely chopped onion
- ¼   to ½ teaspoon Cajun seasoning
- 2   cloves garlic, minced
     Celery sticks, sweet pepper strips, and/or crackers

1. In a 1½-quart slow cooker, combine cream of shrimp soup, spinach, cream cheese, shrimp, onion, Cajun seasoning, and garlic.

2. Cover and cook on low-heat setting for 2 to 3 hours. Stir before serving. Serve with vegetables and/or crackers.

Per ¼ cup dip: 103 cal., 8 g total fat (5 g sat. fat), 40 mg chol., 290 mg sodium, 4 g carb., 1 g fiber, 5 g pro.

Spicy Sausage Pizza Dip

*If you're lucky enough to have any of this spunky dip
left over, spoon it into freezer containers and stash it in
the freezer to enjoy later. It will keep for up to 3 months.
When you're ready to serve it again, thaw it in the
refrigerator and reheat it in a saucepan.*

Prep: 25 minutes
Cook: 5 to 6 hours (low) or 2½ to 3 hours (high)
Makes 28 (¼ cup) servings

- 1   pound bulk Italian sausage
- ⅔   cup chopped onion
- 4   cloves garlic, minced
- 2   15-ounce cans tomato sauce
- 1   14½-ounce can tomatoes, undrained, cut up
- 1   6-ounce can tomato paste
- 4   teaspoons dried oregano, crushed
- 1   tablespoon dried basil, crushed
- 2   teaspoons sugar
- ¼   teaspoon cayenne pepper
- ½   cup chopped pitted ripe olives
     Assorted dippers (such as toasted bread slices sprinkled with Parmesan cheese, breadsticks, breaded mozzarella cheese sticks, and/or sweet pepper strips)

1. In a large skillet, cook sausage, onion, and garlic until meat is brown and onion is tender. Drain off fat.

2. In a 3½- or 4-quart slow cooker, combine sausage mixture, tomato sauce, undrained tomatoes, tomato paste, oregano, basil, sugar, and cayenne pepper.

3. Cover and cook on low-heat setting for 5 to 6 hours or on high-heat setting for 2½ to 3 hours.

4. Stir in olives. Serve with assorted dippers.

Per ¼ cup dip: 70 cal., 4 g total fat (2 g sat. fat), 11 mg chol., 275 mg sodium, 4 g carb., 1 g fiber, 3 g pro.

Spicy Sausage Pizza Dip

This **zesty** sausage party pizza relies on toasted **Italian bread** for its no-work crust. For mess-free serving, cut the **pizza** into appetizer-size pieces that **guests** can pick up easily.

Pizza by the Yard

Horseradish-Crab Dip

Here's a knockout addition to any appetizer buffet—a cream cheese, mushroom, and crab dip that's perfectly seasoned with horseradish, Worcestershire sauce, and smoky bacon.

Prep: 15 minutes
Cook: 1½ to 2½ hours (low)
Makes 10 (¼ cup) servings

- 2 6- or 6½-ounce cans crabmeat, drained, flaked, and cartilage removed
- 1 8-ounce package cream cheese, cubed
- 1 4-ounce can (drained weight) mushroom stems and pieces, drained and chopped
- ¼ cup finely chopped onion
- 2 slices bacon, crisp-cooked, drained, and crumbled
- 2 teaspoons prepared horseradish
- 1 teaspoon Worcestershire sauce
  Rich round crackers and/or celery sticks

1. In a 1½-quart slow cooker, combine crabmeat, cream cheese, mushrooms, onion, bacon, horseradish, and Worcestershire sauce.

2. Cover and cook on low-heat setting for 1½ to 2½ hours. Stir before serving. Serve with crackers and/or celery.

Per ¼ cup dip: 223 cal., 14 g total fat (6 g sat. fat), 57 mg chol., 426 mg sodium, 14 g carb., 1 g fiber, 11 g pro.

Pizza by the Yard

If you like, sprinkle on some sliced olives for more flavor.

Prep: 20 minutes
Cook: 5 to 6 hours (low) or 2½ to 3 hours (high)
Makes 20 to 24 servings

- 2 pounds bulk Italian sausage
- 1 26-ounce jar garlic and mushroom pasta sauce
- 2 large green and/or red sweet peppers, chopped
- 1 1-pound loaf Italian bread, split lengthwise and toasted*
- 1 8-ounce package shredded pizza cheese (2 cups)

1. In a large skillet, cook sausage over medium heat until brown. Drain off fat. In a 3½- or 4-quart slow cooker, combine sausage, pasta sauce, and sweet peppers.

2. Cover and cook on low-heat setting for 5 to 6 hours or on high-heat setting for 2½ to 3 hours.

3. Spoon sausage mixture over toasted bread. Sprinkle with cheese.

Per serving: 264 cal., 14 g total fat (6 g sat. fat), 39 mg chol., 608 mg sodium, 18 g carb., 1 g fiber, 12 g pro.

*Note: To toast bread, preheat broiler. Place bread, cut sides up, on a baking sheet. Broil 3 to 4 inches from heat for 3 to 4 minutes or until toasted.

Candy Bar Fondue

Candy Bar Fondue

A small slow cooker doubles as a fondue and melting pot for this irresistible chocolate sauce that starts off by melting a candy bar. Although highly unlikely, if there are leftovers, reheat and serve over ice cream.

Prep: 15 minutes
Cook: 2 to 2½ hours (low)
Makes 12 servings

4	1.76-ounce bars chocolate-coated almond nougat bars, chopped
1	7-ounce bar milk chocolate, chopped
1	7-ounce jar marshmallow creme
¾	cup whipping cream, half-and-half, or light cream
¼	cup finely chopped almonds, toasted
2	to 3 tablespoons almond, hazelnut, or raspberry liqueur (optional)

Assorted dippers: sugar wafers, pound cake cubes, strawberries, cherries, and/or pineapple pieces

Finely chopped toasted almonds, toasted coconut, miniature semisweet chocolate pieces, multicolored candy sprinkles, and/or almond toffee pieces (optional)

1. Combine nougat bars, milk chocolate, marshmallow creme, and whipping cream in a 3½-quart slow cooker.

2. Cover; cook on low-heat setting for 2 to 2½ hours. Stir until smooth. Stir in the ¼ cup almonds and, if desired, liqueur.

3. To serve, transfer chocolate mixture to a 16-ounce slow cooker, if desired; keep warm on low-heat setting. Spear dippers with fondue forks; dip into chocolate mixture, swirling as you dip. Dip into finely chopped nuts, chocolate pieces, sprinkles, and/or toffee, if desired.

Per serving (fondue only): 294 cal., 16 g total fat (8 g sat. fat), 25 mg chol., 55 mg sodium, 34 g carb., 1 g fiber, 3 g pro.

Apricot-Glazed Ham Balls

Here's a slick trick for uniformly shaped meatballs: Pat the meat mixture into a 6×5-inch rectangle on a piece of waxed paper. Cut the meat into 1-inch cubes, then use your hands to roll each cube into a ball.

Prep: 20 minutes
Bake: 20 minutes
Cook: 4 to 5 hours (low) or 1½ to 2 hours (high)
Makes 30 meatballs

1	egg, beaten
½	cup graham cracker crumbs
2	tablespoons unsweetened pineapple juice
1	teaspoon dry mustard
¼	teaspoon salt
½	pound ground fully cooked ham
½	pound ground pork
½	cup snipped dried apricots
1	18-ounce jar apricot preserves
⅓	cup unsweetened pineapple juice
1	tablespoon cider vinegar
½	teaspoon ground ginger

1. For meatballs, in a large bowl combine egg, graham cracker crumbs, the 2 tablespoons pineapple juice, dry mustard, and salt. Add ground ham, ground pork, and snipped apricots; mix well. Shape into 30 meatballs. In a 15×10×1-inch baking pan arrange meatballs in a single layer. Bake, uncovered, in a 350°F oven for 20 minutes. Drain well. In a 3½- or 4-quart slow cooker place cooked meatballs.

2. For sauce, in a small bowl combine apricot preserves, the ⅓ cup pineapple juice, vinegar, and ginger. Pour sauce over meatballs.

3. Cover; cook on low-heat setting for 4 to 5 hours or on high-heat setting for 1½ to 2 hours.

4. Serve immediately or keep covered on low-heat setting for up to 2 hours. Gently stir just before serving. Serve with toothpicks.

Per serving: 86 cal., 2 g total fat (1 g sat. fat), 15 mg chol., 151 mg sodium, 15 g carb., 0 g fiber, 3 g pro.

Apricot-Glazed Ham Balls

Holiday Wassail

Holiday Wassail

Wish your guests the best of the season by toasting them with this spiced fruit and brandy sipper.

Prep: 10 minutes
Cook: 4 to 6 hours (low) or 2 to 3 hours (high)
Makes 16 (6-ounce) servings

6	inches stick cinnamon, broken
12	whole cloves
6	cups water
1	12-ounce can frozen cranberry juice concentrate
1	12-ounce can frozen raspberry juice blend concentrate
1	12-ounce can frozen apple juice concentrate
1	cup brandy or rum
⅓	cup lemon juice
¼	cup sugar
	Orange slices and orange peel curls (optional)

1. For spice bag, cut a 6-inch square from a double thickness of 100-percent-cotton cheesecloth. Place cinnamon and cloves in center of square. Bring up the corners; tie closed with kitchen string.

2. In a 4- to 6-quart slow cooker, combine the water, juice concentrates, brandy, lemon juice, and sugar. Add the spice bag to juice mixture in cooker.

3. Cover and cook on low-heat setting for 4 to 6 hours or on high-heat setting for 2 to 3 hours.

4. Discard spice bag. If desired, garnish with orange slices and orange peel curls. To serve, ladle beverage into heatproof cups.

Per serving: 178 cal., 0 g total fat (0 g sat. fat), 0 mg chol., 12 mg sodium, 37 g carb., 0 g fiber, 0 g pro.

Index

Index (continued)

Better Homes and Gardens®

{ Whether you're looking for timesaving recipes, a simple no-fuss meal, or a wide variety of options, Better Homes and Gardens® books have the answer.

A great way to experience the taste and variety of America's favorite cookbook brand. }

Fast Fix Family Food has more than 200 family-approved, quick and easy recipes to please everyone in the family.

5-Ingredient Favorites is full of recipes for everything from appetizers to hearty main course meals—all with the flavor of home cooking.

365 Last-Minute Meals features 365 delicious, fast recipes that make it easy to answer the never-ending question "What's for dinner?" with a meal everyone will love.

Available where all great books are sold.

Meredith® BOOKS

ADT1019_0308